The World of Dolls

by Maryanne Dolan

Published by

 **krause publications**

700 E. State Street • Iola, WI 54990-0001

Book design by Amy and Todd Quamme, Design Solutions, Hazelhurst, WI.
Cover photo of Victoria Ashlea Originals by Bette Ball is courtesy of Goebel, Inc.

Please call or write for our free catalog. Our toll-free number to place an order or obtain a free catalog is 800-258-0929 or please use our regular business telephone 715-445-2214 for editorial comment and further information.

Library of Congress Catalog Number: 98-84094
ISBN: 0-87341-570-1
Printed in the United States of America

Dedication

To Mom, Gram, Aunt Frances, and Aunt Molly.
Thank you for all those Christmas dolls.

Acknowledgments

It is a special joy to have friends so willing to share.
You have my deep gratitude.

Susan Batchelor, Cabbage Patch Kids dolls

Rosemary Chambers, bed dolls

Concord Auction Studio, Concord, CA.

Robert Shields, Crolly dolls, Donegal, Ireland

Carol Daniel, Darling Dolls, Carson City, NV

Curt Eberling, Goebel North America

Dee Dee Gardiner, Contemporary Consignment Dolls

Irene Dick, bed dolls

Althea and Ken Garcia, Master Jacks, Livermore, CA

Patricia Gettle, paper dolls

Virginia Gordon, mini Pleasant Company dolls

Lorena Hess, Alaska Fur Enterprises, Anchorage, Alaska

Ed and Sharon Kolibaba, Honey & Shars, Seattle, WA

Betty Krueger, collector

Georgia Kraatz, doll furniture and accessories

Nancy Laurenovic, Modesto, CA

Patricia Le Page, tin dishes, furniture

Maryann Lyons, Lyons Collectibles, Walnut Creek, CA

Dorothy Mallot, Oriental dolls

Maryhill Museum of Art, Goldendale, WA

Hortense McGee, doll collector par excellence

Jan McLean Originals, Dunedin, New Zealand

Ann Olmstead, Original Art Dolls, Woodland, CA

W. Harry Perzyk, Original Sculpture, Sacramento, CA

Pleasant Company of Middleton, WI

Jackie Robertson, Nancy Ann, Storybook Dolls

Rosie D. Skiles, Japanese Friendship Doll researcher, Lafayette, CO

Jack Soares, Girl Scout Dolls

Mieke L. Thorson, Denver Museum of Miniatures, Dolls and Toys

Sue Todd, doll artist, Dunedin, New Zealand

Robert Tonner Doll Company, Kingston, NY

Rosalie Whyel Museum of Doll Art, Bellevue, WA

Note: Photographs of Lyndon Johnson, Barry Goldwater, Charles Lindberg and John Wayne are by Charles Backus and courtesy of Rosalie Whyel Museum of Doll Art, Bellevue, WA.
Photographs of Théâtre de la Mode are courtesy of Maryhill Museum of Art, Goldendale, WA.
Photo of the most recent Girl Scout doll is by Jack Soares, San Francisco Bay Girl Scout Council.

6

Contents

Preface

This book is not necessarily about the greatest dolls ever made, although some of them here may very well be. It is not necessarily about the most beautiful dolls ever created, although that, too, may be. Nor is it even about the most gorgeous costumes ever designed, but in this book there are some that surely are.

Some of the series dolls, and many of the individually designed and marketed dolls, are perhaps among the most beautiful and most elegantly clad ever seen.

This book is intended not so much as a price guide, for who could ever tell a true doll lover what a precious doll is worth—there is no such possibility. There are, however, selling prices on the secondary market, which are a pointer to what a given doll may be worth to any particular group of collectors.

The older, established "magnificent" dolls have had secondary prices firmed by auctions. We think we know what a desirable Jumeau or a scarce Bru may bring because they have been turning up at auctions for many years. But here again, these are only educated valuations and have

nothing to do with the passion of an individual collector who must have a particular doll–high bid or not.

More and more, we have seen auction prices going well over the estimate because of the emotions involved. But for the most part, here we are discussing newer dolls whose pasts are not so long and whose futures seem rosy indeed–even though they are still not firmly established, insofar as secondary market prices are concerned.

Prices are certainly important. My experiences on a call-in radio talk show prove that the number-one question to any collector of anything is, "What is it worth?" No one can tell you that. What it is worth to you is intangible–in the love it projects, in the pleasure it gives, in the satisfaction you feel in owning it. But there are heirs and others who have bought dolls for various reasons and about which they have no deep feelings and they, indeed, should know what it is worth.

I have not attempted to value each doll. Some pictures in this book are truly priceless and historic and included for their informational impact. Others are listed at issue prices and still others at today's actual selling price which is in no way an arbitrary figure, but reflects a selling price which the vendor felt fair–based on cost and other factors a dealer needs to consider. This is as reliable a selling figure as any auction price, which can vary from sale to sale and literally from day to day.

The fact that the older, very grand dolls are literally out of reach of today's collectors is now an established way of life and most of us do not consider them as collectible. This has paved the way for a wave of the most talented, tasteful designers of dolls ever before known. Part of this is the great demand for dolls, one of the country's largest hobby categories, so we need many skilled designers to satisfy this craving.

Another aspect of dolls is their importance as playthings–toys if you will–a concept being lost in the collecting world, and we have to thank some of the new designers, too, for reinventing this phase of doll collecting.

The dolls we love and the things made for these dolls continue to fascinate us with a mysterious lure. It cannot be only the doll; it cannot be only the lovely costumes she wears; it cannot be the little tea sets and small furniture, although they do mesmerize. What can it be?

Perhaps it is memories and a passion for translating these wonderful things into a past. That past may or may not have embraced these things, but we all fantasize about our childhoods–and for us girls, dolls played a large part in our dreams.

Basically, though, we are now dealing with a collector's world. The lavish, utterly impractical costumes of some of the Barbie dolls, for example, do not lend themselves to much handling. True, you could line up Barbie and have a fashion show Paris could never duplicate, but at the same time, it is now becoming evident the doll is again becoming a plaything. You can watch young girls cuddling Sabrina or Felicity as they shop with their mothers, and you will be somewhat surprised and so pleased in a fundamental way that the doll has come home again.

Take a look at old postcards or photographs from the early 1900s featuring young girls and their dolls. It is a lesson in pride of ownership and care-giving (rarely do you see a doll in less than excellent condition) and shining out of the eyes of these girls pictured is love–love for the doll, surely (notice the price of place the doll takes in the photograph). Twenty years hence, that love of the doll will be tied to the love for the giver of the doll as well, and the happy memories the gift awakens.

You are not just collecting dolls: You are creating joy for yourself and those around you, and you are certainly building everlasting memories.

Collecting dolls is like entering a magic place.

Welcome.

Introduction

Dolls are a microcosm of all that has happened, and is happening, in segments of what used to be considered the feminine world.

Until fairly recently, the male doll has been a rather minor part of doll making and collecting, but that is changing–now most manufacturers regularly include male dolls in their repertoire.

There have always been boy dolls, but the increase in their numbers is but one commentary reflected accurately by the doll world on the changes in our continuing unfolding culture.

As dolls become less important as regular playthings and the world of newer collectible dolls assumes major status, the boy doll is becoming a larger part of the field and finding a large marketplace.

This is of great interest: In very early times, some figures we consider "dolls" were stylized versions of humans without much definition. Consequently, some museum curators still debate the form of what we call "doll."

The origin of the doll is still shrouded in mystery since some authorities on antiquities deny that what we term a "doll" today was actually made as a plaything, and was instead a sacred and ritualistic object–an icon.

Figures found in Egyptian tombs, which had been buried with the deceased to accompany him/her on the final journey, were for a long time thought to be dolls. The Greeks had jointed figures with typical hair and dress details, and probably the doll as we know it owes its origin to the Greeks. The Greeks, after all, really knew what they were about.

But it is almost academic to argue the history of the doll as a plaything since history tells us that almost all cultures, in all times, have provided some sort of small figure to interest the children.

The American Indian tribe, the rather mysterious Hopi, for example, would use figures as icons, then pass them on to the children to use as playthings.

The intriguing question becomes, "What actually is a doll?" Categories abound: stuffed dolls, figural dolls, carved dolls, bisque dolls, composition dolls, wax dolls, personality dolls, character dolls, contemporary dolls, and vintage dolls. These categories were at one time finely drawn; now collections include every kind of figure and they will be referred to as a doll collection—and why not? After all, if you are collecting for pleasure, that is an admirable goal—buy whatever pleases you no matter where it fits into the framework of someone else's rigid definitions.

But there is no doubt that doll collecting has changed from its original cozy, sharing, comfortable world to a plateau where doll prices have risen so astronomically it makes collectors wary of publicly sharing their treasures. Where once the collector may most often have been a mature woman, that circle has enlarged to include about 40 percent men and many children—both boys and girls—who can now be seen at doll shows making their own choices.

So, as the world has changed, so has doll collecting. It's really the attitude that governs this field—that lost feeling that this specialty was so unique it was not involved with money; it was emotion. There is still that, of course, because dolls inevitably, and without effort, provoke emotion; but overall, the attitude is different. Any long-time doll appraiser and most serious collectors are aware of these nuances.

No matter, really, because the doll is here to stay and in the process will continue to spread happiness and beauty to those who cherish it.

The field is now so broad, the choices are almost limitless. Where once the vintage dolls, the Bru and Jumeau, and their like, were the goal of every collector, we have now entered a phase where, although they are still considered gems to be admired and perhaps even coveted, they do not seem to be in the real world for most everyday collectors. They are rather like a Tiffany Lily Lamp, lovely and valuable, but average collectors wonder where they could safely place it. Taking care of a great doll treasure today involves much thought and consideration—and money.

So it is with these magnificent old dolls. They have become unaffordable to the average collector and most of us are realistic enough to say to ourselves, "Oh, so beautiful, but let me be sensible. What do I like that I can really afford?"

Thus, the new world of doll collecting: the contemporary designer dolls; the classic stuffed dolls; the dolls from the 1960s; the fun personality dolls; the ethnic dolls; the new reissues of older dolls. The any-kind-of doll that appeals to your mentality that you can readily go out and buy (even trolls are now a big thing). Otherwise, you will probably deal with frustration on a high level, which negates the primary function of any collectible—happiness without too much stress.

Any long-time doll dealer will tell you "the field has changed." The collectors are younger, more men are involved, there is more money available, and more collectors are well informed and very definite about what they want. And, of course, there is the tremendous impact of selling designer dolls on TV shopping networks.

Materials have changed, too. Porcelain is still a desirable medium and we know from dolls that have survived for literally centuries that bisque is a dependable, durable material for dolls. What is now in question is the longevity of vinyl, of which so many dolls have been made. There is some evidence that early plastic dolls are changing: their surfaces are becoming somewhat "sticky."

A 1995 Reutgers story out of England laments "sad doll disease," which is causing deterioration of older plastic dolls. The cause of this "disease" is low-quality iron posts attaching a doll's eyeballs, which react with the plastic head to release acetic acid.

Some doll collectors were terribly concerned about this report; however, it seems it is entirely curable.

This is not a legitimate concern to most of us, but be sure of quality when you do buy an expensive doll, whatever the material, and be sure to get that money-back guarantee.

If your ultimate aim is profit, your motive for buying is entirely different from that of the collector and requires a different mind set. Specialization is your best route here. Take into consideration the beauty and quality of the doll, as well as costume; the name of the artist; the integrity of the manufacturer; the staying power of the seller; the number of any limited editions; and, if you are that careful, the number of your doll in relation to number made.

These, of course, are collector dolls, and some are beginning to garner appreciable profits on the auction market, so check auction sales figures if available—and as you move around admiring the wonderful dolls, be aware of prices on the secondary market. This marks you as a responsible, intelligent collector and if you note price fluctuations in your records' book, you will ultimately be able to make wise choices for yourself and your heirs will certainly thank you.

However you classify your collection, there is no doubt that in the United States, dolls as playthings gained wide acceptance after World War I. The years before that "war to end all wars" were the golden era of the incomparable doll.

During the years when the great doll makers of Europe were producing their masterpieces, this country was not yet involved in the doll market in any sort of competitive way. Of course, we had dolls. There have always been dolls, but no really large-scale manufacturing threatened the European dominance.

The Brus, Jumeau, Simon and Halbig, Marseille, some Kestners—all are commanding historic prices at auctions. They are disappearing into private and museum collections and we tend to look at them now as we might consider an Old Master painting; we speak of them in hushed tones—so beautiful and so unaffordable.

But doll collectors are a resilient lot and the younger they are, the less impact the old magnificent dolls have on their collecting psyche. "Do you have any story-book dolls available?" is a more likely question put to dealers today. Dealers and collectors alike have to accommodate what is available and affordable—and just possibly more fun.

The era of the legendary dolls was a time long before woman asserted complete independence, when little girls were taught all the "feminine" crafts when their mothers, for the most part, were complete homemakers and few worked outside the home.

Little girls were little women and played with and took care of their dolls the way their mothers took care of and played with their daughters. It was the time of the traditional family: father went off to work each morning and returned each evening, and their roles were totally structured. The shortage of early boy dolls testifies to the role males assumed in this picture. Teachers were, for the most part, women; business tycoons were males.

Dolls have played a unique role in the lives of little girls. They have had a subtle, but important, influence and we can trace our social history through our dolls.

The doll has always been a teaching tool, although neither manufacturers nor buyers considered it as such. The clothing of early dolls was so sumptuous, ordinary girls could not have owned such wardrobes; but these garments unconsciously taught a sense of fashion, of good workmanship and materials. They taught elegance and many of them survive in good condition after all these decades because girls handled them carefully, in part because of their great beauty and costume. "Awesome" might just be an accurate description of some of these dolls.

My grandmother, who had traveled to Europe with her parents before World War I, returned with a superb small collection of incredible French dolls. Many years later, I inherited this collection and have never forgotten the feeling of being enveloped in this world of sheer magnificence. Somehow, the collection disappeared, but my original feelings toward it can be evoked by a stray thought or a bit of conversation, or even a color or a beautiful dress. After all, that is what is really important–the great joy those dolls left behind. We lament their loss; we bless their having been. It is a time warp, and we are happily ensconced in it forever.

*A hand-colored postcard of a young girl and her Christmas dolls.
The card dates from December 1911.*

The World of Dolls

The "War to end all Wars" took its toll on Europe generally and as we moved into the 1920s, the affects of that war became evident. Most of the great European doll factories suffered complete devastation from bombings, which destroyed their ability to ever again produce the quantity and quality of pre-World War I dolls. Those companies, which survived the horrors of that war, had to contend with such crippling inflation that many were forced to close their doors.

Not only did dolls in the grand manner wither, and to all intents and purposes die, the world itself changed dramatically—and with it the rapidly evolving role of women as they moved into the larger world and the manufacture and collecting of dolls changed. Subtly, but surely, a new kind of doll was born and as time passed, a new kind of collector.

With the decline of the well-known European doll factories, the American manufacturers stepped in to take over the doll-making world and fill the gap. In the 1920s and 1930s, such firms as Effanbee, Ideal, American Character Horsman,

Madame Alexander, and, of course, others not so well known, took over the doll market and manufactured some outstanding dolls which have well stood the test of time.

Many have, in fact, become collectors' prizes. Those companies, which have survived over this long period, have undergone reorganizations and mergers, and have been acquired by new groups—all the vagaries which overtake older business enterprises. But most of the great names survive, even if in a different form.

The 1940s in the United States were a curious, highly emotional time. Signs of individual patriotism were everywhere. While war waged abroad, the United States was almost totally involved. Men and boys went off to war; women went to work in the factories and at the end of that terrible war, the traditional male-female roles were forever changed.

To the little girls approaching puberty, dolls were no longer the number-one priority. There were many other options girls could consider besides that of full-time mother and homemaker. These changes did not occur overnight, however.

Dolls continued to be available and popular, but never again would they dominate in the same way the list of toys that girls longed for with such a passion.

The very essence of the doll as we knew it changed. The extraordinary Brus and Jumeaus, with their stunning beauty and magnificent materials and clothing, gave way to dolls made by Sears Roebuck. Most of the doll company names we recognize today were active, and even Woolworth's got into the doll act. Its doll sales were quite brisk in this period.

Some impressive dolls were sold through catalogs. One shown in this book was bought because her wig color almost exactly matched the auburn shade of the recipient's own hair color. These dolls were a part of the larger scene and many of them still survive in good condition–unlike some of the older dolls that were well used because they were relatively inexpensive.

Original clothing is often missing or damaged and in many cases we do see crazing, which may mar a quite lovely face. Crazing, cracking in composition dolls caused by too much heat or dampness, is becoming a repairable problem; techniques are improving all the time, so don't despair if your dolls suffer this affliction.

These dolls should be coveted. They were great bargains, but as with all USA products at that time, the manufacturers always felt quality was important.

The products of the other companies active after World War II have gained enormous popularity. Some of them have completely passed from the doll world, although their dolls live on. Some have changed ownership many times, with a consequent difference in quality during some periods. Very few have survived intact as they were then.

The impact of Barbie

But the fateful year 1957 changed doll collecting forever. Barbie was born–full blown and sexy–and while controversy swirled around this leggy, provocative figure, profit margins began to soar. Barbie was a hit. Mattel was rescued and the world became divided into two parts: BB and AB–Before Barbie and After Barbie.

The basic Barbie was manufactured for about a decade in Japan. She was adapted from a German doll called Lilli, purported to have been originally marketed for adult men, and perhaps this is responsible for that ultra sexy look of early Barbie. It is all but forgotten now, but this first-issue Barbie doll did engender some controversy when she was introduced in the United States. Jack Ryan, a prolific designer and a husband of actress Zsa Zsa Gabor, was apparently a key factor in the early adaptation.

The continued phenomenal popularity of Barbie was, and is, dependent on the constantly changing variety of her incarnations and the series mentality. As plate and figurine manufacturers learned long ago, issues in series are almost irresistible to collectors; so Barbie, with her seemingly endless reincarnations and her glamorous self costumed lavishly by famous high-fashion designers, eventually became a trend setter and a thing of such glamour as to be admired for qualities her originators probably never conceived.

Trend-setter Barbie has been an astronaut, a sultry night club singer, a sumptuous Queen of Hearts–you think it, she's done it–and in 1992, Mattel issued a "Barbie for President" doll. No doubt prophetic–somewhere there is a girl named Barbie waiting to grow up and assume that high office.

There is no question Barbie is an icon of the times: girls can aspire to look like her; be like her; achieve as she does; sport stunning outfits the way she does; ride in pink convertibles; make up at lovely little dressing tables; and go off to be Queen of the Mountain or to settle some war in a far-off land–and all the while Ken will be hovering, waiting in the wings.

A lovely lifestyle–and if the girl never achieves any of these goals, she will have had much pleasure anyway. While some psychologists frown on all this daydreaming, that is what Barbie is really all about: anything is possible in the 1990s and beyond for the American girl.

Part of the continuing appeal of the Barbie doll is the feeling she imparts (the costumes are a part of this) that any girl can achieve anything–all the while looking quite stunning. It's reminiscent of early magazine ads: there is the poor overworked housewife vacuuming away, but rather formally dressed and always wearing heels and sporting earrings. Almost none of us remembers our mothers doing housework in such garb, but it's the same philosophy and those ads made for great sales.

So Barbie goes here, there, and everywhere and does everything there is to be done, all the while exuding glamour–makeup in place and dressed to the nines. If dolls are an effective teaching tool, the generation weaned on Barbie will indeed hope to change the world while wearing a Bob Mackie creation. And collectors who acquire these elegantly costumed Barbies will have a rather select piece of American design genius.

Thus Barbie, manufactured cheaply and originally sold for relatively small sums, has become a reflection of the whole United States: she is still going strong; entire large shows are devoted to her; countless articles, even books, have been written about her; museums are dedicated to her; psychologists dissect her influence; and accessories to her many outfits are widely collected. Anything anyone can think of which can be made, has been made; and anything which can be said has probably been said about Barbie.

Now, in 1998, Mattel is updating Barbie body measurements to more normal proportions so she looks more like the girl-next-door overall. No doubt her fans will adjust to that.

It is amazing that the doll-loving public still has the capacity to absorb more. But the Barbie beat goes on and has become almost all things to all people; indeed, Barbie is now much more than a mere doll–the name has worked its way into everyday language and has become generic for a certain look, a certain attitude. She has been everywhere–to the Olympics and Desert Storm; she's been a goddess, a princess, a plantation belle. No wonder we are entranced. No wonder Mattel reports that two Barbies are sold every second.

During the 1997 Christmas season, the newest Barbie was so popular it sold out nearly everywhere and buyers were issued vouchers for redemption when stocks were replenished. For a toy which has been around since 1964, this is incredible.

Barbie must be considered a very large part of the modern doll world, for she is important in the sociological, as well as the economic, context of doll making and collecting. But quickly now, can you think of Barbie's last name? No? She is Barbie Roberts, but just call her Barbie.

One aspect of Barbie is an absolute–should you ever mention this hallowed name, even in the lower reaches of Siberia, not one person will react by asking, BARBIE WHO? Everybody in the entire universe knows Barbie. You would have to go into outer space, where some little green man may not have heard of her yet; not likely, but possible.

In a way, this doll's impact has all been world-shaking and we should all sit down and ponder Barbie. She is one of the most significant dolls of the 20th century.

Artist-designed dolls

But while Barbie is important, she is not all; and as a basic doll, icon or not, she in no way compares with the products of the rising craft of the individual doll artisans.

These talented, inspired people are creating dolls to rival anything ever made in pre-war Europe. Those remarkably beautiful bisque dolls certainly could not be exactly duplicated today at any reasonable price, and given the attitudes of today's children, the wide acceptance of such figures is in doubt.

The old bisque and china heads, even some of the papier-mâché dolls, are beyond beautiful–many are truly splendid works of art, but they have an "other-worldly" appeal. Their beauty and craftsmanship justifies, to some extent, the astronomical prices they command, and scarcity, fragility, and the passage of time continue to contribute to their collectibility. But in 1998, playthings they definitely are not.

As our world changes and moves on, so do dolls and doll makers. Today we are fortunate to live in an era when the doll designer-maker is well respected, and in many cases, acknowledged as a true artist.

Any serious doll collector would certainly have to consider the artist-designer dolls currently being offered if value and investment is the goal. If living with beauty and delight is an equal goal, the variety of offerings by the current doll designers is an opportunity not to be missed. (For a closer look at these dolls, see the chapter on Modern Dolls and Artists).

Beyond playthings

This attraction by collectors to the newer dolls is both understandable and powerful. It is the way of the world for mores to change, for standards of beauty to change, for reasons to collect to change. It is generally called progress.

Indeed, 50 or 60 years ago, dolls were playthings, to be cherished, seated at a small tea table to have the mistress "pour out" tea from a little china teapot into a tiny cup, or the doll would be cuddled in imitation of an adult cuddling a baby; the clothes would perhaps be hand sewn by mother and daughter and the costume adapted to the situation, or the doll would be taken out for an airing in the doll carriage. These sights are not too often seen today, although evidence is beginning to indicate a return to the juvenile tea party, and the older tea sets used by our grandmothers are now commanding very high prices.

The fact that no tea actually came out of that little teapot or the baby doll wasn't responding to the cuddling or cooing didn't matter to the little girl who was wheeling it in the small carriage and adjusting a lacy cover over it. All of this was a fantasy land where imagination was rife and certain kinds of dreams were born.

Now, TV, the VCR, and the Internet have replaced imagination and day dreaming is not encouraged. Can you visualize Marilyn Monroe being cuddled, gently covered with that lacy robe and being wheeled about in a wicker doll carriage? Not readily, but it is more than apparent that part of the world was waiting for Marilyn–she is considered a desirable doll and collectors snap her up.

Some of the Marilyn Monroe dolls are well done and costumed in a spectacular way. In many cases, the facial features are also exceptionally true to life. It was amazing to me to hear of a theft in which several such Marilyn dolls were stolen from an antiques shop that was exhibiting them for their costumes and not primarily as dolls. Many expensive antiques were not touched by the thief, who only wanted the Marilyn dolls.

At that time, these were new dolls; the passage of years, however, has justified the judgment of the thief. Marilyn's popularity in general has become legendary and so her doll representations have also become more collectible and expensive.

Many companies have jumped on the Marilyn bandwagon. There are many such dolls available and still being produced, and in this special category of personality dolls, Marilyn is a genuine star of this genre and will command very high prices.

Her enormous impact continues, as does the collectibility of other celebrities, but even these have not erased the desirability of dolls to be cherished for other reasons: sheer human attraction, admiration toward a particular type, or even more basic—a doll which can be cherished or mothered. Thank heaven for little girls who have such different wants.

While it may be déclassé to discuss this subject, the fact is many new would-be collectors are intimidated by the cost of some dolls. Some young collectors cannot afford many of the new ones, so when the price is reasonable and the doll is presented in something other than a complete doll-oriented setting, we can expect to see new collectors. Surprisingly, many of the newer, most beautifully designed and costumed dolls are reasonably priced for what they are. Even Madame Alexander's creations are now being marketed in less traditional ways. This kind of merchandising attracts people to the hobby who have not been doll collectors or may not have had any occasion to visit doll shops or shows.

As doll collecting moves into the 21st century, we are also forced to think about Beanie Babies (what to think about them is a private matter). Some retired figures have sold for $7,500 and more, but the future is uncertain. They are not dolls, but as a collectible, they are reminiscent of the initial Cabbage Patch Kids' madness—and they certainly are fun.

When you peruse the doll publications or visit shops which feature dolls, think about the doll which attracts you. It surely must evoke memories of some kind, and that is all important. For certainly part of collecting dolls, or even buying one doll you fall in love with, is connected to memories.

Recently I overheard the following conversation at a doll exhibit: "Oh look," said the first lady, pointing to a lovely large doll. "She looks like Catherine."

"Well, a little bit," said her companion, "but the hair color is not quite right; she does look a bit more like Claire."

"Oh, mama," said the little girl with them. "I don't think she looks like Catherine. I think she looks like me." The ladies laughed.

I took a second look—the doll did, indeed, look somewhat like the little girl, but she also reminded me of a little friend none of those ladies had ever seen. It was the doll's expression.

This is an intriguing slice of doll life, and even though I did not hear the outcome of the discussion, it is symbolic—each lady of whatever age had different opinions of that one doll. A doll is not only a thing of beauty (and beauty is certainly in the eye of the beholder), but a reflection of ourselves. We tend to imbue our favorite dolls with qualities we admire.

Of one doll, four opinions–all of them affectionate, all of them ready to embrace the aura of the doll itself. There is really nothing else in the collecting world which inspires such personal interaction.

Museum-quality treasures

This same sort of reaction applies to dolls which many consider more as figures or sculptured dolls, but regardless of what they are called, this new type of doll is beginning to figure largely in what we admire and buy. Museums are partial to these new doll makers and their creations, since, in many cases, they are true works of art.

The new sculptural dolls by doll artist W. Harry Perzyk of Sacramento, Calif. are an excellent example. They are so well done, so stunning, people literally stop in their tracks to gaze at them. (For a closer look at Perzyk's work, see the chapter on Ethnic Dolls).

This is a different effect from the one produced by a darling baby doll–this is an admiration of sheer talent and artistry represented by one figure. To own one of these dolls would be like owning a prized work of art. They do not have the same effect as that baby doll–you will certainly never want to give it a spontaneous hug–but you will admire and be proud of it.

The faces are so inspiring, they spring to life as we look at them. You know instantly this is a treasure of museum quality, not to be cuddled, but to be esteemed. Some day someone will stand in front of a museum exhibit and say, "Oh, how wonderful." And this is the time for us to look about, see the unusual, and take advantage of such opportunity when we ourselves might own museum-quality dolls.

Not for everyone, these dolls attract a totally different audience from the admirers of Barbie or the American Girls Collection–an adult audience. Today a large segment of the doll-collecting world is a mature one.

Diverse doll choices

The doll world is constantly evolving and continues to surprise.

The choices available today are very wide and diverse. From the tiny to the life size, the collector can decide which best suits the individual taste and pocketbook.

Since so many dealers in dolls have lay-a-way plans, which, incredibly, are interest free–and one of the better bargains anywhere–it becomes possible to add to a collection fairly painlessly. Higher-priced dolls must always be considered an investment; it is a rare doll today of almost any era which cannot command some profit when sold. But the aim of the collector is always to satisfy an inner yearning for beauty, emotional appeal, elaborate costuming, or sheer nostalgia. And never forget what a particular doll may represent in terms of lifestyle and personal fulfillment.

The large framework of doll collecting has narrowed considerably for most collectors because of the many newer dolls by talented artists, by the great numbers of personality dolls being introduced all the time, by the rise of the ethnic doll, by the sale of all dolls propelled by home shopping, and by the scarcity driven prices of the old dolls–so specializing becomes a way of life.

These factors have opened the field to so many new choices, it is a collector's dream world and it has also become a profitable pastime because almost any doll will appreciate in value, even if in a small way.

Raggedy Ann and Andy are cases in point. For many years, the darlings were ignored, languishing in shops and baskets of low-priced dolls; but suddenly Ann and Andy have become fashionable again. They are being reissued by many manufacturers, children still love them, and even serious collectors add contemporary, hand-crafted new dolls to their collections.

A friend, who some years ago began her collection as a purely altruistic rescue mission of abused and discarded Ann and Andy dolls, bought them for a pittance, and repaired and redressed them. It became her hobby and now she finds herself the keeper of valuable Americana, more than a doll–a genuine icon of childhood.

So the basic advice remains sound, even if it sounds trite: almost any doll of any age is collectible and will probably at some time increase in value. You may never retire on your profits, but you will definitely not lose money.

The changing face of doll collecting

Collecting dolls of all kinds is one of the most popular hobbies in the United States. It is estimated that the market is as high as 60 percent, but this figure is entirely variable and depends on what publication you are reading.

What is more important is that it is attracting a younger audience with very eclectic tastes. The impact of TV selling, such as home shopping channels; heavy direct-order promotions with beautiful catalogs, which in themselves should be collectibles; telephone selling from highly selective lists; the many specialized doll shops; and now some series doll being promoted from manufacturer's shops in malls–all of these give the buyer a wide range of sources from which to choose.

The Internet is still an unknown, although many collectors are already buying and selling this way. What effect its widespread use may have on prices, dissemination of information, or the quantity of any given doll in circulation is still open to question. It will certainly change things, but to what extent we don't yet know.

Basically the same old adage applies: buy what you like. Any doll should bring joy to the owner; it should satisfy some inner need, a need which we all share, to look at something we own and feel a sense of pleasure, even of peace. That should be anyone's foremost reason for buying any doll.

Having stated the obvious, it is wise to remind all collectors that the guidelines for collecting for pleasure, as well as possible profit, comprise several factors: No matter what the area of collecting, always buy the best example of your collectible which you can afford. If you purchase expensive dolls, consider first the workmanship: does this doll meet your criteria for good manufacturing? Is it jointed so that it moves easily? Is the doll marked clearly with the artist's name, the number of the edition and the number of your doll within the overall number issued? Are the eyes–and the eyes are important in dolls–well set in the doll or are they painted on? And, of course, condition, condition, condition. In the newer dolls, the box can be important. And mint in box is becoming the catchword in all collecting fields including dolls. So is your doll in pristine condition?

What comes into play here is not necessarily your attraction to the dolls, but possible future appreciation of the price you paid. As with any expensive item, always get an itemized receipt outlining exactly what your purchase includes.

Does any of this matter to you? Do you just love that particular doll whether she needs a new bonnet or not; whether she is missing her original socks and shoes? If you can just not live without her as she is, then buy her, find what you need to restore her (a great justification for haunting the doll shows), and let some unknown descendent worry about "mint in the box."

Caring for your dolls

Take a few sensible precautions with the dolls you collect. Early composition dolls require a bit of looking after. Do not use water to clean any composition doll; moisture is to be avoided at all times when storing them—no basements with their damp, moist cold or heat—and do not place your dolls in direct sunlight.

Most doll collectors realize this and do take care, and although these "unbreakable" dolls are not totally so, they will develop crazing, sometimes to such an extent that a doll is disfigured. There is hope, however, and today doll restorers can do wonders to conceal such defects.

Acid-free paper is also a must. Any good doll museum curator can make recommendations to you concerning the use of such paper. It is relatively inexpensive and you can purchase as much or as little as you need. Be sure to use this for packing extra costumes.

It is wise for any doll collector to make use of the large public museums which boast doll collections. A conscientious curator should be glad to (and can) help in many ways, and likewise, a conscientious reference librarian in any public library should be equally cooperative in helping with any doll research you may wish to do.

Always consider researching your dolls. Little tidbits of information keep coming to the fore and while not world shaking or changing what you already know, they may shed new light or an inter-esting aside perhaps on your collectible. It is amazing how much new information is surfacing, partly because of the Internet, with its many knowledgeable users willing to share. The world of information is becoming so wide, so fast, we almost cannot keep up. But keep trying.

A 'priceless' hobby

So, doll collecting can be all things to all collectors. It is not really just "collecting," it is a way of life. It is also a continuing treasure hunt, with who knows what wonder may be lurking in the next shop.

There are things every good collector already knows or should know: do not equate price with value, they are not the same; condition is a very big factor and almost all dolls today, unless of unusual rarity, are priced according to condition; and "mint in the box" for any doll after the 1960's is almost the norm.

If you buy collectors' dolls, you will certainly depend on the reputation and skills of the artist. The costume is becoming more and more important and the choices are so vast you can let your imagination run riot; but while dreaming about the doll itself, check the clothing for tailoring details and the over-all look. The doll should be well marked, have visual appeal, at least to you, and, of course, you should love it beyond price.

A good doll collection also needs to be appraised by a qualified appraiser, and such an appraisal should be in writing. The collection should also be insured, so save all documentation. Naturally, a doll collection should be included in the collector's will.

Doll collecting, except on a small scale, has gone beyond the "fun" stage. It should bring great joy. If it does not, if you are buying for investment, the whole attitude must be different. It is then on the same scale as buying stocks or investing in commodities. We who love dolls for themselves sometimes forget we are competing with others who look at these little treasures and think "investment."

If you are already dedicated to the hobby, you need no reminders of the joy it will bring, or has already brought, into you life. New places, new people, new horizons; if you are just entering this wonderful world of dolls, you have before you a lifetime of happiness you could never have envisioned. You are on the road to fulfillment and your life will never be the same.

Thank the doll gods for that.

American Girls

Probably nowhere do consumers have so much input in a doll line than with the American Girls Collection.

Dolls in today's American Girls Collection are ones whose looks, names, and accessories are solely chosen by the consumer, says The Pleasant Company of Middleton, Wis., which makes and markets them.

The dolls have up-to-date accessories, which include a rollerblading package, a Girl Scout uniform, and a mini computer–that really is up to date.

The company has enormous potential for growth, since it regularly adds a new doll, really a new character, to its line; and, of course, the accessories keep pace with new developments on today's social scene.

Young collectors never seem to have enough of these dolls and their impact has been huge. There is a genuine love affair between each owner for her doll, and because of the networking among other owners, there is affection for others in the group. It's a rather unique relationship and quite heartwarming.

Emotions aside, these are wonderful dolls. They are attractive, well made, and there is an ease of handling and changing wardrobes which is unusual. The ready-made backgrounds provided with each doll also add a whole intriguing dimension.

Collecting the necessary accessories that go with dolls is not new, but many of the current doll lines, such as American Girls Collection, emphasize this aspect. Of course, in today's market, it is not essential to own the basic doll in order to collect the accessories, but American Girls has tied the accessories very tightly to each of its dolls.

The wonderful thing about such marketing strategy, as the American Girls Collection series represents, is the historical aspect. The dolls come with books, which teach early history so entertainingly, and costumes, which show the clothing in context of the times. It is a marvelous concept and done quite consciously with learning in mind, which makes this delicate, subtle approach all the more important.

The Pleasant Company was founded by Pleasant T. Rowland, an elementary school teacher who began using her own

A family portrait of "American Girls of Today" dolls. One of the interesting things about American Girls, as everyone seems to call these dolls, is this feeling that owning a doll engenders. Several young people have confessed to feeling almost part of an extended family. The various meetings, projects, newspaper, and other ways of coming together fosters this strong connection between dolls, their owners, and other girls who also own one or more. As the photograph illustrates, the choices of a type of doll are not endless, but so carefully chosen that almost every admirable doll of any particular period is available.

materials in order to bypass what she considered a "lack of creativity and excitement" in the classroom textbooks. A trip to Williamsburg in 1985 inspired her to produce the American Girls' line of dolls, books, and accessories. The success of all the American Girls' products, sold only by catalog, has been phenomenal and they now have a secure place in the doll world.

The Pleasant Company says it is "A line of books, dolls, and accessories designed to give girls seven and up an understanding of American history and to foster pride in the traditions of growing up female in America."

Read that and then think back to the early years of the century. There was very

little advertising connected with the stunning German dolls, and no one ever questioned the exact place of the little girl doll owner as a potent future influence, nor was her future as a driving social and political force in any way connected to her Christmas doll.

Her world was circumscribed–her Christmas Kestner just emphasized it precisely. The recipient was a small adult, her doll was dressed in a copy of the utterly exquisite clothing of a chic adult, and the doll represented not only her plaything, but what place she herself would take when she "grew up." It was all relatively simple.

But collectors of today who love American Girls' Samantha or Molly McIn-

Addy Walker© is 18", with a soft cloth body, poseable arms and legs, and vinyl head. She has a marvelous wig, which you are invited to brush with a wire wig brush. Her large brown eyes open and close. She wears a striped dress of cinnamon pink (a delicious description of a color). Addy's story is one of Civil War days. The 1998 catalog price for the doll and hardcover book is $82.

Samantha Parkington© is a child of the Victorian years, an orphan being raised by her wealthy grandfather. She, too, has "sparkling brown eyes, which twinkle as they open and close." She has long curly hair, a soft body, and poseable limbs, including her head. She is wearing a checked-taffeta dress, with a matching hair bow, long black stockings, and black strapped shoes. She measures 18". The 1998 catalog price for this doll and hard-cover book is $82.

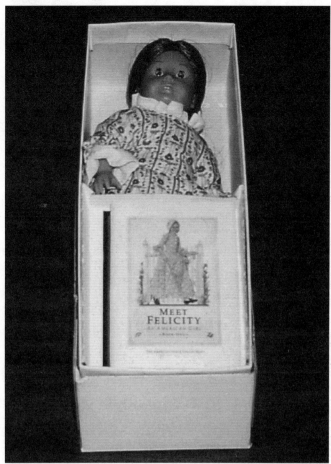

The dolls pictured here and on the following two pages are the "mini" version of the American Girls Collection. Issued in 1995-1996, these are 6" tall, and small versions of the regular 18" collection. The book, the first book of Kirsten's, has very readable print in this mini version. These are no longer available through the catalogs. Value of each "mini" American Girl doll is $95-$145, but this price is rising.

tyre are creatures of a culture no doll maker of the 19th century would have understood. Their new dolls represent their dreams, as dolls always have, but in a way guaranteed to give the girl owner feelings of pride not only in the doll itself, but in her manufactured history. The young owners of these dolls get painless lessons about colonial history, the days of the hardy pioneers, the Civil War years, Victoriana, and the significant World War II era. As the dolls' creator puts it, "We give girls chocolate cake with vitamins."

This is, in fact, a marketing dream, which benefits everyone. The dolls are appealing and manufactured to "exacting standards of historical accuracy, aesthetics, and quality." Not only does each doll meet these standards, but so do the accessories, the books, and the miniature dolls as well, which are all crafted to correspond to the activities mentioned in the books.

The dolls' vinyl heads and cloth bodies measure 18 inches and since children love interaction with their toys, each doll has legs and arms "which can be posed any way the child wishes." A characteristic of these dolls is their beautiful faces, which are not just an empty beauty but life-like, with an intelligent look.

There are very popular clubs built around owning one or more of these dolls, a bi-monthly newspaper, a pen pal club, and, what else in 1998, but an interactive web site all its own.

Interactive is, indeed, the key word here–on all levels the doll owner is encouraged to learn, create, and, oh joy, to meet with other owners to work together on projects, exchange ideas and generally trade information and, of course, to have fun. Not a grand new idea perhaps–after all, girls together with their friends have always played with dolls. What is different is that growing up in our culture has changed, and continues to change; in fact, it is much more complicated, and this "coming together" is an altogether new thing–more organized and more international, but still the focus is the doll and the experience she stimulates.

The whole idea is monumental in its expression of what dolls are all about. Regardless of their stunning beauty, or their interest as figures, dolls have always been a teaching tool–how to mother, how to study fashion, how to sew, how to play nurse or teacher, and, in the American Girls' series, we have seen the ultimate manifestation of integrating a toy into a lifestyle. The latest addition to the family is Josefina, a Hispanic girl of the Southwest.

Because each doll is relatively expensive and the accessories are many and also rather costly, the owners of these dolls seem to take excellent care of these toys and respect the integrity of what they are meant to be. This 10-year-old company has sold more than 3,000,000 dolls and is an interesting commentary on other types of dolls, which attract different audiences and do not seem to impact lovers of American Girls' dolls. This is truly a wonderful time for doll collectors and proves that variety is, indeed, the spice of life.

A most telling fact about these dolls is that collectors who haunt thrift shops, consignment shops, and various kinds of sales, where other collectible dolls may occasionally turn up, report that an American Girls' doll has never surfaced. What a wonderful testimonial to the place these particular dolls hold in the childhood psyche of the 1990s' real American girl.

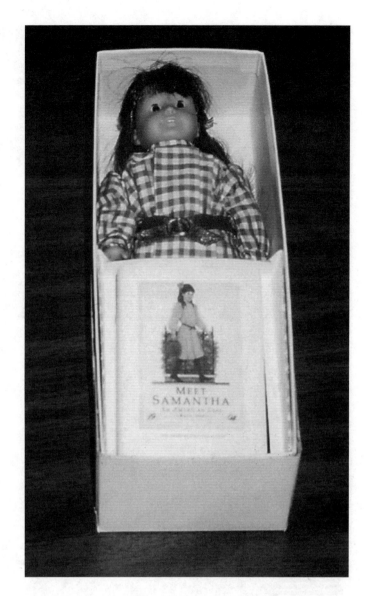

Bed Dolls

All collectors do not relate to all dolls, which is wonderful, and why we have such variety to choose from. An unusual doll, which at first may take some attitude adjustment, is the bed doll or boudoir doll.

To get into the mode, you have to transport yourself to another time and another world, to a place so far removed from us today it takes a giant leap–the 1920s and 1930s. You would have walked into an ultra-feminine bedroom in, say, 1928; a pink satin spread covered the Art-Deco bed, and lo and behold, a strange long-legged creature, also pink, stared back at you, cigarette dangling from painted lips, ash blonde wig slightly askew. The whole concept is so out of context in 1998, and that is part of the great charm of these rather odd fancies.

The bed doll of the 1920s is an example of a long-neglected collectible doll. One collector I know seeks these avidly, not because the doll itself may be charming and a great decorative accent, but because, as she says, "My favorite aunt always had a pair of these draped on her satin bedspread. I loved her and these dolls remind me of her and her love for me. As I've found more of them, I've grown to appreciate them for what they are."

So many new collectors are attracted to this field and there are numbers of them making their own bed dolls. It is not terribly difficult, even without a pattern, but in the time of their greatest popularity, McCalls actually sold patterns for sewing your own, which was great fun if you had any artistic skill and could hand paint the face in an original way.

Still another collector of bed dolls recently told me she wished she had lived during the 1920s. "I'm a born flapper," she laughed, as she showed me a new acquisition: a turbaned, feathered, and beribboned long-legged bed doll, cigarette in mouth, and posed provocatively on her bed. "Isn't she something?" she asked.

Yes, indeed, she is. She also represents with absolute accuracy the period of the Roaring '20s so popular today. So here is a doll which is delightful, unusual, and so reminiscent of a particular period of history as to be considered almost definitive. If ever you want to see the 1920s brought to

life, view a bed-doll collection.
It's uncanny.

These are one of the fastest-rising categories of doll collecting. Aside from their whimsy, they can be quite beautiful dressed in silks and satins and laces. Their painted faces and elongated bodies are like no other doll, and after being sadly neglected for many years, they are back and their bedroom eyes lure new fans every day. It is difficult to understand where the many, many bed dolls have been hiding. They are certainly not understated. No doubt condition has kept many off the market and to the dedicated doll purist, a minus is the fact that they cannot be absolutely attributed. Lendi did make a foray into this market, though.

The bed dolls with glass eyes are becoming highly sought after, but those with painted eyes have a primitive appeal rather like early American paintings, where the most untrained of itinerant artists emphasized this dominant facial feature. The painted eyes often have a sly, come-hither look, which to the current collector is unique. After all, said a recent newcomer to this field, "I've never heard such an appropriate name—this bed doll actually does have bedroom eyes."

There is nothing quite like the old bed dolls, which are still underpriced and undercollected, but rising on both counts. Many of the boudoir dolls we find are American, although unmarked in any way, but some very elaborately dressed and decorated examples originated in France and Italy.

There have always been collectors of these dolls, but not on any grand scale.

They are often found in poor condition and if you buy these with damaged clothes, a capable seamstress or a professional restorer should do body, repair, and

This is an authentic bed doll of the 1920s, with a restored wig. She has been carefully and accurately re-dressed in green chiffon. Value, $175-$225.

A variation of the bed or boudoir doll is the Lamp Doll. This beauty, c. 1920, is one of a pair. She wears a taffeta dress trimmed with original lace and is composition with a wire frame. She is quite lovely and a testimony to a lost era of boudoir elegance. Value, $450-$495, the pair.

often had molded faces covered with stocki-net, but most had features painted on and this accounted for the various seductive looks. It is like coming upon a hidden treasure to find a boudoir doll in original clothes, perhaps with its original hat and jewelry.

You need a sense of humor to collect boudoir dolls. Looking at them stirs strong feelings. Bed dolls, probably more than any other artifact (without any effort on their part except to look languid), evoke a feeling of a time everyone seems to yearn for–and a strong expectation that some dashing flapper twirling her long beads will come slink-

These two dolls do not have the elongated figures of the usual boudoir doll but they were being offered at a large doll show as original bed dolls. The faces are typical and they could be twins. The tag on one doll reads, "Boudoir doll, Red Riding Hood," and on the other, whose name is "Blossom," the tag also reads "Boudoir doll." Both are a 1920-30s' original and each value $395.

restoration. Choose restoration as a first option rather than replacement, and salvage all possible original clothing.

Many of these dolls have the clothing stitched to their body, which can be of composition or can be cloth over wire, or stuffed or padded within a sateen or similar type body. The higher-priced creatures

The bed dolls on this page and the following one are part of a collection begun fairly recently. They wear original clothes, and show the wide variety within the genre. It is an amazingly varied collecting field and some of these dolls are beautiful, with incredibly elaborate costumes. Prices are uneven, but the starting price of any bed doll in good condition and with original clothes should be around $295, but prices are probably rising as you read this. The doll pictured above is of either French or Italian origin. The doll pictured at right is made in the way of the bed doll, but is actually a tea cozy.

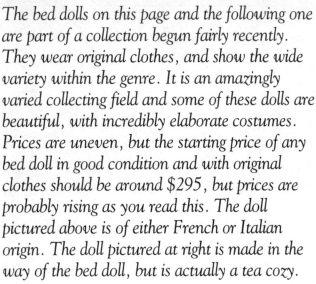

ing through the doorway. This feeling seems to prevail even if you were born in 1955–the flapper is an everlasting symbol, the eternal vamp, and everyone knows her.

Prices have not stabilized completely. Condition is important and, of course, original clothing is a factor, even if not perfect; but surprisingly, some newer collectors feel that faces and the bodies themselves, except where stitching may be required, are more important. Any clothing on the doll is a genuine plus, and collectors are willing to buy "as is," which is wonderful because this adds to the preservation of this rather endangered species.

This type of doll, in rough condition, usually sells for $95 to $165. The pristine examples are in a much higher-priced category and prices thus far are completely variable. Any fine bed doll in excellent condition should have a beginning price of about $295, but marked examples with glass eyes can cost $1,000 or more.

Cabbage Patch Kids

The day began as any other, except for the hordes of excited people waiting in line at a local discount store, where some were "trampled" in the rush to get a new item being offered.

Nowadays, people recall the sight with some awe as if it were an historic moment, and in the world of doll collecting it was, for the frenzy was over a doll—a rather unusual-looking doll called the Cabbage Patch Kid.

If you are like most of us, you have a strong reaction to Cabbage Patch Kids: either you love them passionately, or you can certainly live without them.

One thing is absolutely true, though, regardless of your first reaction: these dolls have a tendency to grow on you. When you see a collection, you realize the attraction. They are soft and cuddly; they each have an identity, which gives them personality; and their birth certificates and adoption papers make each doll seem important and special.

These dolls were such a sensation when introduced in the early 1980s that shoppers made spectacles of themselves clamoring for them at local discount stores. The Miami Herald described one such mob scene as a "stampede," and photographs in other newspapers across the country testified to the pandemonium the dolls' introduction created.

In Concord, N.H., more than 300 shoppers from three states suffered biting winds and cold to get to the store selling these dolls; not all succeeded, however, and an official news report said police were called to stop any trouble that erupted over the frenzy to get these Cabbage Patch Kids.

Today, they are readily available. Prices on less-than-perfect figures have plummeted, and others can be found without their original clothes and other accouterments. The original figures wore clothes that their creator says he bought from other vendors at markets, and baby clothes will often fit the dolls. This is an excellent time for any collector to be buying these orphans, since some dolls have more than held their value and lately there is a new trend building for harvesting in the Cabbage Patch. Buy them now when you see them, nurture them, and wait.

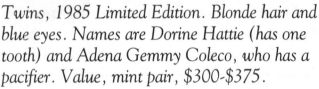

Twins, 1985 Limited Edition. Blonde hair and blue eyes. Names are Dorine Hattie (has one tooth) and Adena Gemmy Coleco, who has a pacifier. Value, mint pair, $300-$375.

Young Astronaut, 1986, Coleco. Her name is Gabie Angeline and she has two teeth (on bottom), dimples, short blonde hair, blue eyes, and the ability to hold things in her hand. Comes in a space capsule with an American flag, poster, brochure, and document. Also has a helmet and in-flight patch. Value, $225-$275.

Xavier Roberts, who developed these "kids," says he always felt he should start small and dream big. He called his dolls "little people" and no two are alike. They carried adoption papers, but no price tags. The very earliest babies were not hand stamped, and are now scarce and valuable. The Scandinavian Cabbage Patch kid is one of the rarest, but only the writing on the box and adoption papers indicates that it is not American.

Roberts considers himself an artist, but his business acumen is not to be denied. His experiences at flea markets and craft shows with his sculptures in clay eventually led to the Cabbage Patch and a licensing agreement in 1982 with Coleco, which became, at the time, one of the biggest toy

licensers in the world. In 1985, the company reaped $600 million. By 1986, it was losing money, attributed to "not being able to manage its booms and busts." Coleco began in 1932 as a leather-products company and over the years had many successes, as well as failures, but overextended into the Cabbage Patch field and found it had harvested nothing but trouble.

As the company continued to lose money, these "winsomely ugly orphans" lost popularity. When Coleco closed in 1989, Hasbro became the new licensee of these dolls.

Dedicated collectors never lost faith,

Talking Kids, 1987, Coleco. Text on boxes reads, "They react when you touch or talk to them. Holding real conversations with other kids, they 'understand' each other and even hum a tune together. They come with a cup and even take a drink." These kids used advanced computer technology, which does not require tapes. These are certain to be big winners and even now value has risen to $300-$400. Pictured here are Ema Zara, left, with red cornsilk hair, brown eyes, one dimple, and a blue velvet dress; and Philomena Augustine, who has black corn silk hair and brown eyes. She wears pink.

Brown Cabbage Patch Horse; dolls fit very firmly on saddle and can "ride the horsey." Prices are not stabilized. Value, $75-$150.

however. They kept their dolls and their optimism, and are now being rewarded.

The genuine "kids" boast the Xavier Roberts' signature on their bottoms, a belly button, and the Official Adoption Papers. The release of the "kids" (Roberts has been quoted as saying, "Don't call them dolls, please") spawned clubs, limited-edition figurines, buttons, and tremendous enthusiasm not very often equaled in the doll world.

The Cabbage Patch Kids were a phenomenon: they appeared, they conquered, and then the initial frenzy passed and they have settled into a niche of their own. As an historical footnote to the doll-collecting world, it is important to note that it was just that–an almost mass hysteria. It defies explanation and it is difficult in retrospect to encompass the madness exhibited by grown men and women over these dolls. As they say, "You would have had to be there."

There are vast collections of these figures dwelling happily with their original owners and in truth they are becoming very endearing and appealing to a whole new set of collectors.

Cabbage Patch Kids have reached a new plateau; some have sold at auction for more than $2,000, while others remain in lower price ranges. If any given doll is still in its original box and boasts various original accessories, any selling price will reflect the higher value dictated by these amenities.

Definitive collectors interested in rarity and investment possibilities look for dolls with red hair, rug hair, freckles, and pacifier: these are considered valuable assets to any Cabbage Patch kid in terms of both collectibility and monetary value.

The Cabbage Patch has grown larger and the harvest is getting a bit more difficult. In 1997, an advertisement for a "Family Reunion & Adoption Event" held in Georgia Mountains Center in Gainesville, Ga., invited "Come meet

This blue-eyed girl has cornsilk curls, gold hair, one tooth, and dimples; her hand can also hold a brush. Her name is Libby Dorothy Coleco-1986. Value, mint, $95-$150.

This foreign Cabbage Patch Kid, along with the two on the following page, were sold in boxes with all text written in the language of their particular country. Ruschel Kinder of South Africa, above, has blonde hair, green eyes, freckles, and a dimple. Value, $300-$350.

'Mildred' one of the earliest Little People re-adopted for $20,000." You may well gasp.

These "kids" have been collected for a long time now and we are beginning to understand the attraction these dolls held for the original owners.

Even the names given these dolls are unusual and Roberts, their creative daddy, was certainly an innovator.

Pictured here is Bamboline of Italy. She has red hair, green eyes, freckles, and a pacifier. Value, $200-$250.

This Kid is from Mexico and hit the market in 1984. She has rug hair, blue eyes, freckles, and a pacifier. Value, $195-$250.

Character and Personality Dolls

After the demise of the European doll manufacturing operations, the dolls made in America became more realistic and the character and personality dolls became a large segment of the field.

Cartoon characters, particularly, were fodder for doll makers and today they are worth a small fortune if found in good-to-excellent condition. They speak to us in subtle ways—of innocent fun; of good times with family. I can recall quite vividly my great aunt exhibiting her Skippy doll, from a cartoon drawn by P.L. Crosby. She said it had been given to her as a birthday gift in 1931 and began a lifelong doll collection. Although she was not concerned with this doll's pedigree, she did, indeed, have the Effanbee 1929 all-composition Skippy. At quite an advanced age, she still had Skippy and talked about the doll and its meaning to her in the most exuberant way. She dearly loved Skippy.

A rather shabby Skippy was selling at a recent doll show for $450. Who can say if that very doll had once belonged to my great aunt? Dolls are like that—their attractions lie not only in their beauty and elegance or overall appeal, but in their associations and memories. Skippy was certainly neither beautiful nor elegant, but, ah…what memories she created.

The personality or celebrity doll has achieved such status for several reasons: Americans are totally fascinated with prominent people no matter the basis for that popularity; the usually low issue price; quality; and availability.

For a long time these dolls were not costly and could be bought for so much less than a good old bisque doll, which was a big factor in their collectibility.

The secondary market abounds with celebrity figures, so if you missed them when they were first introduced, there is a chance of finding what you want now. This is a field driven by sheer nostalgia. You can pick your celebrity from any avenue of entertainment—sports, music, theater, and, of course, movies. It's such a broad field, the hunt for these dolls is relatively easy because so many shops deal in the new collectibles.

These dolls have appreciated in value to such an extent that for some years now, many large doll companies have manufactured and marketed them through every possible medium—newspapers, magazines (specialty and general), radio, TV, and mail order.

Most of these dolls can be recognized instantly if you have ever seen an image of the subject before. The artists who craft these, especially the later ones, are skilled and sensitive to expression, as well as features.

It's rather uncanny. When an Elvis doll stands there, guitar at the ready, you almost expect to hear that "Hound Dog" howling.

Madame Alexander has crafted many celebrity dolls, including English royalty and the Dionne Quintuplets. Some of these dolls have generic faces and can be identified only by their tags; but the age of the doll does influence this market, and a vintage Madame Alexander is always desirable. Her Theodore Roosevelt has the advantage of being a well made and costumed male doll and her first ladies dolls are becoming incorporated into the rapidly expanding first lady memorabilia field (more information on these dolls is at the end of this chapter).

If you are historic minded, this kind of collection can really be a history lesson. Most presidents have been cloned in composition or vinyl and some of the depictions are incredible likenesses. If such figures do not raise your partisan risibilities, this can be an interesting way to collect. A doll of General McArthur, for instance, recently turned up to complete a military diorama for a military-history collector who is not a doll person at all, but was thrilled at his find. The First Ladies dolls also have moved into this category. The costumes are often elegant and usually represent an important occasion on which a particular dress was worn.

This set was made by Effanbee for Sears. It is the "Most Happy Family," and includes mother, girl, boy, and baby. Each child has their own box clearly labeled "Sister" and "Brother" within the heart. Mother is 21", and wears a typical 1950's costume–pill box hat perched on rooted vinyl hair, skirt, bolero, and blouse, all are striking in vivid red and white. She is fully jointed, as all mothers need be, and in the style of the period, even wears stockings and high heels. Notice the rings she wears. The all-vinyl baby, also fully jointed, is 8". Brother and sister are a bit taller, 10", but they, too, are jointed and all vinyl. The sister has rooted hair; the brother's is molded. Effanbee simply took Fluffy, Mickey, and Tiny Tubber and turned them into a full-fledged family. This set is so indicative of the role dolls can play in the evolution of fashion, nothing could be more definitive of the times, clotheswise; 1958. Value, $350-$450.

48

Several versions of Shirley Temple; singer and actress Deanna Durbin, top; and second from left, the much sought after famous figure skater Sonja Henie, with her trunk and costumes.

The Alexander dolls have always boasted fine costuming and the faces are adorable, so we tend to overlook the fact that the face is not truly representative of the person whose image it was created. The tag makes it official, though, and the Alexander trademark makes it valuable.

Most of the well-known doll-making companies made forays into celebrity dolls–as far back as Louis Amberg & Son in 1915 with Charlie Chaplin, to Kaysam's Juliette Prowse in 1961, or Evel Knievel by Ideal in the 1970s, to Marilyn Monroe by World Doll in the early 1980s. Almost no well-known person (and even some relatively unknown) has escaped a doll likeness.

The biggest influence on celebrity doll collecting was the Golden Age of movies, the 1930s and '40s. Almost every star was created in composition or vinyl and those figures are still much sought after. People's memories drive the market. Deanna Durbin and Margaret O'Brien dolls became recent acquisitions to a large collection and the collector's happiness is boundless. She recalls these actresses with such happiness because they were part of her childhood.

Of course, Shirley Temple is queen of it all, never to be dethroned. Probably one of the most admired of all the actors and actresses Hollywood ever produced, regardless of the era, Shirley Temple is an active community leader, an international diplomat, and she has lent elegance and great dignity to the popularity she built as a child star. The numbers of dolls issued in her likeness are almost countless; since her first success, dolls have been issued and reissued by all the great doll companies in her image.

Shirley Temple is in a class all by her adorable self, but she represents a trend that personality doll collectors have long followed: try to collect figures of Hollywood personalities– even obscure ones will amuse you and cannot fail to be sought after sometime in the future. It's all too true, as collectors like to say–any doll you own or any doll you find collectible is important to someone.

Shirley Temple is living history and you can tell your children about her stardom and her later achievements, which is another plus to this kind of collecting.

Another legendary celebrity who has a variety of dolls in her likeness is Marilyn Monroe. Some of these dolls are well done and costumed in a spectacular way. In many cases, the facial features are also exceptionally true to life. Nevertheless, I was amazed to hear of a theft years ago in which several such Marilyn Monroe dolls were stolen from an antiques shop. The shop had been exhibiting these dolls for their costumes and not primarily as dolls, but they were still much more tempting to the thief, who left many expensive antiques untouched.

At that time, these were new dolls; the passage of years, however, has justified the judgment of the thief: Marilyn's popularity in general has become legendary and so her doll representations have also become more collectible and expensive.

Many companies have jumped on the Marilyn bandwagon; there are many such dolls available and still being produced, but in this special category of personality dolls, eventually Marilyn will be a genuine star of this genre and command very high prices.

This is reinforcement of the adages long held by collectors: buy what you like (everyone seems to love Marilyn); keep it in the original box; and if you really love dolls but you also are thinking in terms of investment, try to anticipate trends–then insure your collection and include it in your will.

With access to the Internet spreading so rapidly, that certain celebrity "someone" is now fairly easy to find. Since success breeds success, no enterprising doll maker could ever resist the lure of the well-known TV characters, the easily recognized movie geniuses who made us laugh and cry, and advertising figures which gained prominence both for their companies and for themselves–almost any genre to which the public has reacted has been grist for doll makers.

It has been a hugely successful foray into uncharted waters in many cases, but all in all, the dolls have been successful.

Who could resist Laurel and Hardy, a grinning Lucille Ball, or the adorable, and at the time, totally unique Dionne Quintuplets. They all represent something

Ming Ming Baby with original box, which is a small treasure itself. This was imported gift ware, Quon Quon, and can be considered a scarce item. All mint condition.
Value, $395-$450.

beyond the figure itself; they all represent a time, a moment even, which has stayed with us, has made us smile or remember something precious to us.

The Dionne Quintuplets (all girls) were born on May 28, 1934 in Canada and quickly became international stars. People who recall the birth and early years of the quints feel connected both to the period, the happiness, and the sadness of the family.

Collectors who actually lived through the event itself are becoming fewer and the older representations of the quints in doll form are becoming less available–so the story itself is becoming lost and the dolls are becoming primary.

Young collectors today undoubtedly are probably not even aware of, or particularly interested in, the Dionne family.

Charles Lindberg is in a class all by himself. A genuine American hero, he was the first to fly solo across the Atlantic and the anticipation and frenzied receptions he received on both sides of that ocean has not been rivaled in sheer intensity. He was tall, handsome, and shy, all of which made him a logical target for the media. This doll, whose tag clearly identified Lindberg as "Our Lindy," was made by Regal Doll Mfg. Co. of New York and probably released in 1931. His famous flight jacket is well done and boasts the easily recognized fur trim. While his windblown blonde hair is characteristic, his facial expression borders on the caricature. This, however, is a very desirable doll, since Lindberg has become a big separate collecting field and in the doll world, this is not an easy example to find. Scarce, $350-$395.

John Wayne's popularity as an actor was immense and there are many dolls and other type figures made in his image. This is the second of Effanbee's "Legend" series, which was released in 1982. The tag reads, "American Symbol of the West." The doll is dressed in Wayne's usual western gear. The face is remarkably accurate and the doll does catch the essence of the man. Vinyl, jointed, painted hair and eyes. Current value is $200-$265 and rising.

This is a hard-to-find Arthur Godfrey doll set. Many people may not even remember Arthur Godfrey, although it wasn't that long ago that he was a popular radio personality. Godfrey had his own "gang" and was enormously popular for a long time. Haleloki, one of Godfrey's cast members, is represented here with her lei, Hawaiian guitar, Hawaiian-print clothing, and, best of all, her grass skirt. This is a good example of the collectibility of the celebrity doll–Arthur Godfrey, unbelievably popular for many years, but now unknown to a new generation. Here is a set of dolls, cute and well made, but sold originally on the basis of the name recognition of the celebrity involved. This is a real find from the 1950s. MIB value, $275-$350.

This is an excellent lesson for all collectors–to try to learn the history (several of the quints are still living) and the background of your collectible and put it in a certain period so it becomes much more interesting. It is almost unbelievable how quickly information is lost, so always document everything you can about your purchase and its provenance.

The admirers of John Wayne could tell us about that. The doll made in the image of this prodigiously famous star was quite popular and sold well even when controversy swirled about his politics during the Vietnam War. It is now a highly desirable collectible doll, and very few people recall the rancor.

Even Elvis Presley has his speckled history. To the collector, this is no doubt of little importance, but just think if you were to set about gathering information about him, his times, his influence, his world-wide impact; you would add greatly to your own knowledge and better understand the cult which has grown up and is flourishing around his memory. The collectors of Elvis dolls do that–they all seem to know about him and his period in great depth.

Elvis was the 1960s. Look at enough of his dolls, his figurines, his photographs in all their costumed glory and without even trying, you begin to understand that turbulent period a little better. You begin to understand the controversy he created. Never underestimate your doll's ability to teach you something.

A recent TV program on wild animals featured an eland; this particularly beautiful creature had been named Amanda Blake. It's likely most, if not all, people involved in the show didn't know who Amanda Blake was. Admittedly not a household name today, she was a fairly popular star of the legendary western TV show "Gunsmoke," which ran until 1975.

This proves the average recognition span of most celebrities by their adoring public is short indeed. Given that fact, it is ironic that collecting celebrity dolls has a huge following. It becomes understandable, though, when we begin to look at auction records: In 1994, in Newport Beach, Calif., a Kathryn Grayson doll sold for $10,400. Quickly now, who was Kathryn Grayson? She was a famous actress who starred in

We tend to think of celebrity dolls in terms of theatrical figures, but politicians are also celebrities and becoming big business to collectors. Here are two such dolls: Lyndon Baines Johnson, left, a former president of the United States; and Barry Goldwater, a very well-known senator and aspirant to that higher office. Both are exceedingly well done, properly dressed, and each has an identifying political button. Both also have a definitive facial trademark: Johnson with the heavy eyebrows, and Goldwater with the heavy-rimmed eyeglasses. The hats reflect, with clever subtlety, the Southwest origins of these politicians, as well as making their identification easier since the hats were their trademarks. It is almost impossible to put a definite price on these dolls since they are relatively scarce and that influences the market. They are usually acquired by very avid collectors of certain kinds of figures and not always purchased by doll collectors, so prices are variable. The value of Johnson is $135-$195, while the Goldwater doll has a value of $125-$175.

musicals during the 1940s and '50s.

It is important to buy these dolls when they appear. Their sale life is usually brief. Take, for example, "Charlie's Angels," a very popular TV show which aired from 1976 until 1981. The three original angels, Jaclyn Smith, Kate Jackson, and Farrah Fawcett, are still well known, with Farrah being the one who continues to make most of the headlines. Toward the declining years of the series, I was conducting a seminar and mentioned I had seen these dolls in their original boxes at a local drug store for a minimum clearance price of $1. The minimum was really a giveaway to clear older inventory. I advised all doll collectors in my audience, whatever their preferences, to buy them immediately.

Some students did so and still talk about it because others who waited a few days found that remaining small stock had all been sold, never to be seen again in that setting and at those giveaway prices.

The lesson is well learned, however: the popular life of the celebrity TV or movie doll is brief, one might say ephemeral, and if personalities in doll form interest you, the collector, you have to be alert and ready to buy them when they appear, for their days are numbered. When those days have passed, the canny collector who bought at a low original price has a collecting prize, even if initial demand has slowed or disappeared.

This type of doll seems to increase tremendously in collector interest and almost always appreciates in value.

If you buy personality dolls because you enjoy this type of collecting and are not overly concerned about ultimate profit, the pressure is less intense but the advice is still sound: always try to buy at issue price; in the process, your favorite toy store manager may become your dearest friend and you will have saved lots of money.

Personality dolls are timeless in spite of the fact each character may represent a particular era. Many of today's collectors never saw the film "Gone With the Wind" at the time it was made, but almost everyone recognizes Clark Gable, who played Rhett Butler, and knows Scarlett O'Hara, played by Vivian Leigh. Their images have been recreated many times by many doll companies.

Charlie Chaplin, Skippy, the original Campbell Soup Kids, and more recent figures such as Dr. Spock, Lucy, Elvis, and Bart Simpson—it's a wonderful world, this celebrity doll collecting, dominated only by your own imagination and pocketbook.

Here are a few more categories in the character and personality collecting field that have become popular:

Advertising dolls

Advertising dolls are becoming a factor in the doll market. They are still inexpensive for the most part, easily found, and made of many materials. For example, Pillsbury's small darling, the Pillsbury Doughboy, cost $5 at a recent show.

Planters' Mr. Peanut is already in many collections and in 1993 was created in a newer, very dashing image—slimmer and "contemporized" for the younger collector. Mr. Peanut dates back to 1916 and the older versions are eagerly sought after—classifieds are full of "wanted" ads for him.

And, as strange as it seems, a prestigious maker of Pentium computer chips, Intel, has introduced a series of odd figures as a promotion. This is really up-to-the-minute collecting. Intel has called these figures "The Bunny People" because the Intel technicians wear protective gear called "bunny suits." These technicians manufacture Intel microprocessors in ultra-clean manufacturing environments. The space-age-looking suits protect against contamination and the psychedelic colors of the uniforms worn by these faceless dolls are almost overpowering.

Made in China and issued in 1997, these dolls are 100 percent polyester and intended as playthings since the label reads "ages 3 and up." These figures come in several colors, in two different sizes, can be ordered from Intel or through its catalog or web site, and are surprisingly soft and cuddly.

This doll represents one of the newest entries into the advertising-doll sweepstakes and is proof that we all need to be alert to new collectibles.

Have you used your cellular phone, turned on your modem, e-mailed your broker, scanned the Internet, and faxed your doll dealer today? Doll collectors, too, have moved into the new electronic world.

Any doll representing a well-known company or a product that company makes, is fair game. Look at the Campbell's Soup Kids, who have been so popular for so long they have been reincarnated in a slimmer, low-fat diet look–again an example of the doll world reflecting the changing American culture.

Except for the older already popular examples, this is an excellent way to begin a collection since a younger collector could find many "newish" advertising dolls at low prices.

For example, once a popular children's film with charismatic animated heroes and heroines has been released, had its run, and then become part of the past, the characters, (either in plastic or cloth versions,) become thrift-shop fare, with a consequent low price.

If you live long enough, this collection will be highly valuable; in the meantime, it can be enjoyable, engrossing and amusing, and a great way to interest a child in collecting.

This takes time, of course, and is not for everybody, but it is a good way to pick up bargains for something not yet really collectible, and is also a way of keeping your advertising doll collection up to date.

If advertising dolls are not your fancy and you are unfamiliar with some of the offerings, you would be surprised at the companies which used dolls to promote their wares. Who can forget the Gerber baby? Remember the stuffed McDonald's characters, or the ultimate advertising doll, Buddy Lee, who has achieved star status although he began as an advertisement for overalls?

Most of us do not realize how many once-prominent American companies have disappeared from the business scene. The older advertising dolls, some made by major doll manufacturers, such as Ideal, are now pointers to companies whose names were household words in their day and whose connection to us now remains only in the dolls they used to sell their products.

Collecting advertising dolls, no matter the material, can be a foray into America's sociological past, as well as amusing and fairly inexpensive. The trick here is to keep absolutely current, watch the ads themselves for premium dolls or figures, and do not neglect any kind of sale where you think such dolls have become "clearing out the children's rooms," items. This is a really fun collectible and if you do it carefully, you'll never even have to use your credit card to pay.

Scouting dolls

Collecting all scouting memorabilia has become a popular diversion. Still, many of those collectors profess never to have seen some of the adorable dolls wearing the

It is an interesting commentary on the current doll-collecting scene that many celebrity dolls, including this Elvis, are periodically coming up for public auction in perfect condition and still in their original boxes. This Elvis doll, by World Doll, also has all the original information. It was released in 1984 and is an excellent likeness. Value, MIB, $150-$225.

Jane Withers was an accomplished child actress and played character parts as she grew older. This is by Ideal; $1,500-$1,600.

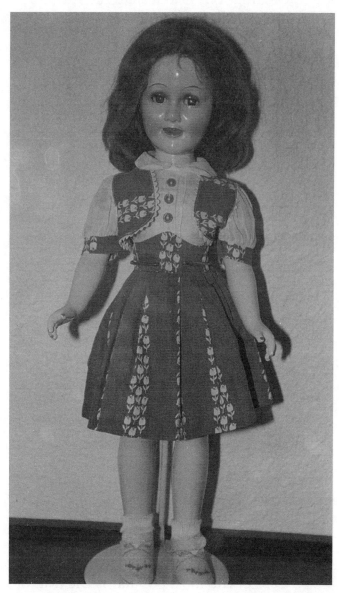

Deanna Durbin, Ideal Doll Co., 1939, original condition. This is a particularly lovely composition doll. Durbin was a fine singer and good actress, but she never reached the stardom of Shirley Temple. The contemporary makers of Deanna Durbin dolls must have admired her, since almost all her doll representations are lovely. Value, $500-$700.

uniforms of Brownies. These are the 6- to 8-year olds whose uniforms were indeed brown. Their doll selves have lately been discovered, with consequent price rises.

Collecting Girl Scout memorabilia is late blooming. Boy Scout material has always been collected on some scale, but the female side of scouting developed later. Juliette Gordon Low of Savannah, Ga. brought the idea back from England and it wasn't until 1913 that the first handbook for girls was written. Many prominent American women have been involved in Girl Scouting and the dolls seem a natural outgrowth of the earlier feminine influence. They are dressed correctly in uniform and are so realistic and appealing you feel almost obligated to buy some scrumptious cookies from them.

First lady dolls

A number of companies have issued representations of the first ladies. The Smithsonian Institute's holiday catalogs have regularly featured them; in fact, the Smithsonian commissioned a set it called "Presidential Wives Series" designed by Suzanne Gibson. Many doll shops and shows have carried them. Quality of both doll and clothing can vary, but almost all are interesting and some of the unmarked dolls are a good investment.

One of the most popular is the doll of Mary Todd Lincoln. In spite of her flawed reputation, Mrs. Lincoln seemed to have had elegant taste and the original of the gown she is most often pictured wearing is in the Smithsonian's collection.
Its color is royal purple, reputed to be Mrs. Lincoln's favorite; it is velvet with white satin piping and lace trim on the bodice and sleeves. The dress was worn to a reception held in the White House on New Year's Day in 1864.

There are new dolls of most of the first ladies. Nancy Reagan's collector's porcelain image is inaccurate as to her coiffure worn on the grand occasion of her husband's inaugural ball, but it is a good likeness of her.

An added facet of this type of collecting is that most of us can actually remember seeing Nancy wearing that very gown during TV coverage of President Ronald Reagan's inaugural festivities. So the doll represents living history, although even now a scholar or fashion follower would probably be the only one to point out the coiffure mistake. When reminded, the manufacturer said it did not intend to correct the hairdo on this doll.

A first ladies' doll collection is easy to begin and assemble and still not too expensive, but obviously the numbers are limited unless you intend to collect figures of all first ladies by all makers.

And so it goes–this can be a wonderful collection and lead to other things. One collector has built an eclectic collection of books written by some of these women, as well as others written about them, and he displays the books beside each figure. This excites quite a bit of additional interest. This particular collector began in the political field and the first ladies have become a tangent.

These women, all so different both in appearance and personality, are a fascinating study. If a doll collection can be said to have meaning, this type certainly does. It can, and should, lead to a study of fashions of the time, happenings of the time (political and otherwise), gossip of the day, mores of the time, and the impact some of these women have had. It's a far reaching and important segment of collecting, as our first ladies assume more prominence and leave more of an imprint on history.

A first lady doll collection is not just

Captain Kirk and Mr. Spock took us into orbit with such finesse, no one who saw them on the original TV series, "Star Trek," will ever forget them. These dolls, still in their original boxes, illustrate the complete "Star Trek" cast, as well as Spock and Kirk themselves in full regalia. It is so helpful when the manufacturer lists all pertinent information as on these dolls–"Manufactured exclusively for the Mego Manufacturing Corp., N.Y., NY. Made in Hong Kong, these are 8" fully poseable action figures." The days when buyers discarded boxes and tags are probably long gone and it is easy to see why they should never be discarded. The information can be invaluable to researchers, collectors, museums, and anyone interested in doll history. Value, Mr. Spock, $145-$195; Captain Kirk, $135-$175. Star Trek memorabilia of all types has been seriously collected for many years. Trekkies sponsor a huge convention, maintain all types of information sources, and keep in touch with each other. Trekkies are a delightful cult, so these dolls have added value as a separate collectible.

the doll itself, but what the doll represents. Naturally, the number of these dolls is growing larger as we all grow older. There are now many such figures available in many qualities and they are made in a variety of materials. Of course, we tend to think in terms of the newer porcelain first lady dolls and they are certainly lovely, but other kinds are available. It does take some searching though.

Madame Alexander issued a set of six first lady dolls, which are now selling in the $100 to $125 price range. Alexander also produced first ladies in a second edition and these range from $85 to $125.

Other manufacturers have issued these dolls in series and there are also unmarked dolls of these women by unknown makers. Any and all are collectible.

Shirley Temple herself, at left, by Ideal; 1950s, original; $800-$1,000. Shirley Temple with her original clothes; value, $1,300-$1,500.

This Shirley Temple rain set, beret, cape, umbrella, and matching galoshes, is not rare, but at the same time, not too easily found. It is really quite imaginatively designed. Value, $195-$225.

One of the seemingly hundreds of new versions of Raggedy Ann and Andy, these were bought in a craft shop and have been redressed by the new owner in modified authentic antique quilts. The pair, bought for $85 in 1995 and then redressed, are valued at $145-$175.

Three versions of Little Orphan Annie, all MIB. At the top is a vinyl Annie by Knicker-bocker; bottom left is a porcelain Annie; and at bottom right is a rag-doll Annie, also by Knickerbocker, 1982. These were made when the Broadway musical "Annie" was very popular. As a doll, Little Orphan Annie is beginning to rival Shirley Temple in her reissues. Value, vinyl, $25-$35; rag doll, $20-$30; and porcelain, $50-$75.

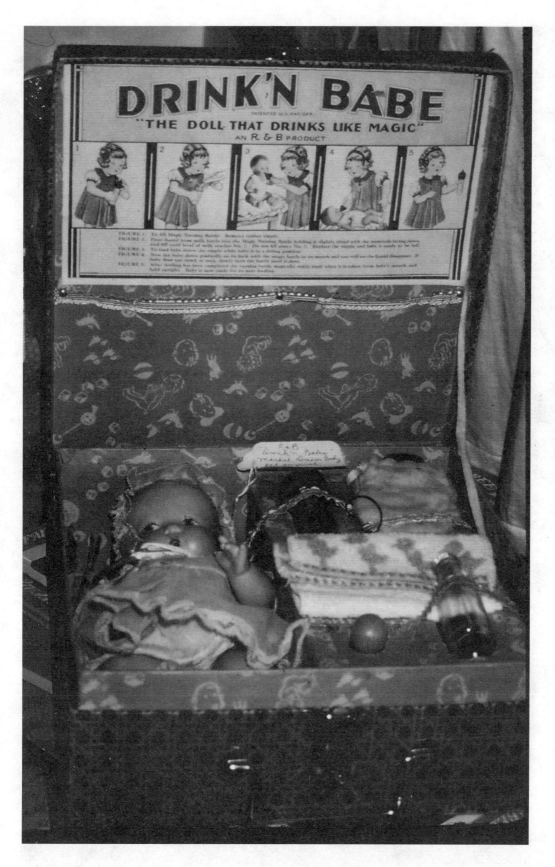

"Drink n' Babe," an R. & B. product, is the doll that drinks like magic. All original in trunk, complete with accessories. The trunk itself is interesting with its original caning on the front panel. Also marked "Dream Baby." Value, 1997, $295-$350.

The Colleen Moore Doll House Doll kit. Excellent condition, all original. Value, $450-$495.

Composition Googly eyed, marked MADE IN GERMANY, 6" tall. Each doll valued at $185-$225. They are posed before a mirrored oak doll's dresser. c. 1900-1915.

Collecting all scouting memorabilia has become a popular diversion. Still, many of these collectors profess never to have seen some of the adorable dolls wearing the uniforms of the Brownies. These are the 6- to 8-year olds whose uniforms were indeed brown. Their doll selves have lately been discovered with consequent price rises.

These dolls are fairly abundant, although not too well known, are still reasonably priced, and among the cutest representatives of any organization or advertiser you will ever see. Brownie and Cadette by Effanbee. Small (1965), has a value of $35-$45. The taller one (1966) has a value of $50-$60.

These Friends of Girl Scouting Family campaign dolls represent an opportunity for collectors of this type of memorabilia to acquire a set of dolls which will not be reissued after the initial order of 1,200 has been exhausted. The dolls are without faces (like the old Shaker dolls) because "every girl is the face of Girl Scouting." The first doll issued was named Julie. A contest was held to name the second, and Savannah was chosen. Each year a doll will be dressed in the uniform of one of the Girl Scout's program levels starting with a Daisy, then a Brownie, a Junior, Cadet, and finally a Senior Girl Scout. These dolls are currently being offered as tokens of appreciation for unrestricted gifts of $50 to the San Francisco Bay Girl Scout Council. If you are a collector willing to support a worthwhile cause, you should have acquired all the dolls by the year 2001.

This First Lady doll of Mary Todd Lincoln is 12" tall and was first sold through a catalog for $69.95, but soon after was selling in some shops for more. The doll cost $75 in 1985. A recent secondary price has been $145-$195.

This Martha Washington doll wears a gown of soft pink faille, with hand-painted floral design and a white lace cap, typically 18th century. The doll, 12" tall, is a Smithsonian Institution issue and rather difficult to find. Value, $150-$195.

Grace Goodhue Coolidge is one of the first ladies about whom we hear little. She was a gracious, handsome, well-educated woman who kept a fairly low political profile. Nevertheless, she made a decided impact with her various interests, and was a rather famous hostess of political breakfasts. Neither of these dolls' faces was intended to resemble the first ladies'. Here is Mrs. Coolidge, with pearls slightly askew. Value, $125-$150. The costume on this doll reflects the fashion era in which Mrs. Coolidge presided over the First Mansion, and is in sharp contrast to the styling of the gown of Mrs. Lincoln.

Presenting the
Lincolns

Raymond Lamb sculpted this magnificent interpretation of Mary Todd Lincoln and Abraham Lincoln for the Series of Living Image Dolls issued by the United States Historical Society. These are based on photographs by Matthew Brady and other contemporary photographers of the Civil-War years. A limited edition of 2,500, they are 12" tall, made in America, and signed and numbered by the artist. Issue price is $975 for the pair; $525 individually. Value on the secondary market is $1,500 the pair; $750 for each figure.

These extraordinary dolls, Thomas Jefferson, Abigail Adams, Benjamin Franklin, and George Washington, from left, have been sculpted by renowned sculptor Raymond Lamb and officially issued by The United States Historical Society. The costumes, authentic in every way, were designed by Susan Sirkis and Nanette Attkisson. The heads and hands are all movable and of fine porcelain. These are limited-edition dolls of 2,500, and all are signed and numbered in 24-karat gold on the back of the neck. Each doll is a hand-made original and carries a 100-year guarantee. These figures are investments in our history and given the research, numbers of people involved in the project, and the meticulous detailed hand work, as well as the genius of the sculptor and designers, this kind of doll could never be made again. For more details of these dolls, write to the United States Historical Society at First and Main Streets, Richmond, VA 23219.

A more modern Peggy Nisbit, this Theodore Roosevelt is, as always, ready to charge up San Juan Hill. Original tag. Actual selling price and value, $100-$145.

Madame Alexander's fame as a maker of dolls which have been collected over a long period of time, does not require much elaboration in any new book. To date, so many books and articles have been written about her and her company, it would be superfluous to recap her career. It is an arresting sight, however, to encounter such a large Alexander collection as recently came up at a local auction. There is an entire book available documenting statistics, names, and dates of manufacture and prices for Alexander dolls. They have all achieved high collectible status and my appraisals involving dolls prove that all earlier Alexander dolls are considered treasures to the collectors. and have certainly proved a good investment.

The photos featured on this page and the one following are a small selection of Alexander dolls in their original boxes. They are among the more than 75 Alexander dolls recently sold at an auction. They are part of the collection dealing only with "Gone With the Wind" figures, such as Scarlett O'Hara, pictured above. Not all are pictured here, but the collector seems to have been especially partial to Scarlett. All dolls had original tags and were in original condition. A rather amazing auction find.

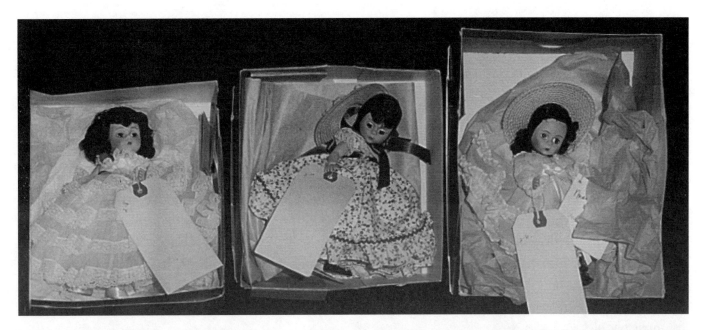

These two pictures were part of an exhibit of the ever-popular Patsy, old and new, at a recent doll show. Patsy continues to be one of the most collectible of all dolls. There are clubs and newsletters, and everything you want to know about Patsy is available somewhere. There are also reissues, which are attracting collectors.

She has a rather old-fashioned charm, and her size and dimensions are appealing. Her costumes never overwhelm the doll itself and best of all, as with some people you have loved, she is the kind of doll we remember with affection and recognize as a friend when we meet her at a shop or show.

Doll shows highlight Patsy; she is that much in demand. Effanbee made her and she was one of its most successful efforts. She was an early-series doll intended to be a doll girls would want to handle and play with, and the clothing was always a plus.

Each of her outfits was well designed and made, but more important, it was absolutely appropriate to the doll and the image the maker was trying to project. At the time Patsy was first released, dolls were considered primarily as playthings; they were not being bought for investment by most people.

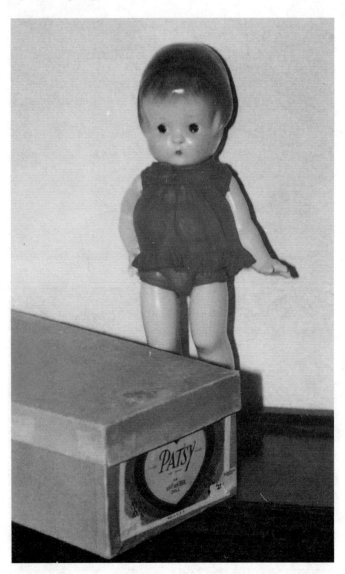

Patsy, with original box and clothing, by Effanbee, 1930s. Value, $450-$550.

A recent doll-show exhibit, one of many featuring Patsy. This photo shows reissues of Patsy, as well as other dolls, paper dolls, and accessories. All this at one booth. A good doll show is an excellent learning experience and you will encounter friendly and knowledgeable dealers. You will also be very apt to find excellent prices.

"Sesame Street" characters, such as Bert, are still popular among today's doll collectors.

Belonging in the "so-ugly-they're-cute category," trolls make a fine addition to any doll collection.

Barbie for President, in the original box, which has never been opened. This was actually bought at Toys "R" Us, the toy store chain for which it was made in 1991. While Barbie is still to some extent a plaything, she is becoming more and more a collector's doll and some never get outside their original boxes. This is somewhat scarce but not rare. It was a limited edition, and inexpensive originally. The box is equally interesting and colorful on the reverse side. Value in original box, $40-$60.

Edith, made by the Rothschild Doll Company-
U.S.A. in 1986, comes with a bear and book.
Wool felt, jointed, hand-painted face, human-
hair wig, white apron, and velvet shoes. An
appealing, well-made doll. Value, $245-$275.

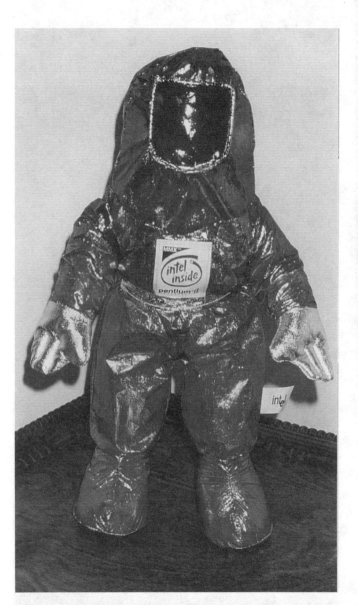

This Intel Corp. technician, wearing a "bunny
suit," is a good example of an advertising doll.
Dressed in varied psychedelic colors, blue,
green, and pink, this is a must for the advertising-doll collector or the soft-body doll collector.
Retailing for $12 in the company catalog in
1997, it now has a value of $20-$25.

Meagan, produced by Edwin M. Knowles
China Company, was designed by Cindy
McClure. All porcelain with jointed neck,
arms, and legs, she wears a pink and white
voile dress and pink overskirt. The white shoes
have been taken off to show the details of the
sculpted toes. She holds a picture book.
Ashton-Drake Galleries, 1989; $500-$700.

This Lenci doll is made of pressed felt and has a
hand-painted face. She's wearing a yellow felt
dress, blue hat lined in yellow and felt shoes,
and has the usual side-glancing eyes; 1982;
$500-$700.

Martina, Great American Doll Co., by
Rotraut Schrott, 1988. All bisque. Custom-
made glass eyes, human-hair wig, and lifelike
modeling. Exquisitely dressed. Value,
$895-$1,200.

Long-faced Jumeau by Janice Cuthbert, 1989.
Bisque head, jointed body, with jointed wrists,
blue paper-weight eyes, and Mohair wig. Pale
pink velvet dress and bonnet lawn petticoat;
$600-$800.

Lady Di Bride, 16", Royal Doulton by Nisbet.
Reads, "Her Royal Highness Princess of
Wales." This is No. 2,610 of the edition of
3,500; $900-$1,500.

Gorham's "Little Mary" (of lamb fame). She is
a musical doll and 16"; 1985. Value, $400-
$500.

Holly Hobbie by Gorham, 12", 1986. Calico dress with leg-o-mutton sleeves, beige apron, laced brown boots, bisque head and arms, soft body. Marked Zazan R. 84. While Holly has increased in value, she is still way undercollected and undervalued at $195-$250.

This look-alike Patsy Ann is 16"; $225-$300.

Lennox Victorian Doll "Amanda," made of bisque. She wears a taffeta dress and is 16"; 1984. Value, $600-$800.

Jan Hagara, vinyl "Cristina" with Christmas bear, hand signed. The doll wears a beige lawn dress, blue underskirt, blue ribbon sash, lawn bonnet, and brown wig. In original box with hang tag; 1984. Hagara vinyl dolls are somewhat scarce. Value, $650-$850.

Kindergarten collection, Marjorie Industries Inc., by Marjorie Spangler. A copyrighted original creation; 1980. Each is 16". Jessica, right, is dressed in brown cotton. Douglas has velvet pants, velvet hat, and beige shirt. Value for the pair, $600-$700; individually they are $350-$395.

At left is Tansie Comes to Visit, 1986, by Patricia Coffer. The doll is 10" and made of bisque, with a soft body. Mohair wig, coral coat, white socks and shoes. Georgetown Collection. Value, $350-$450. The other doll is "Beatrice" by Monica Mechling. All muslin doll and clothing, painted face, blue eyes. Teddy is also muslin. These are the last cloth dolls Mechling made before turning to bisque doll making. Value, $450-$600.

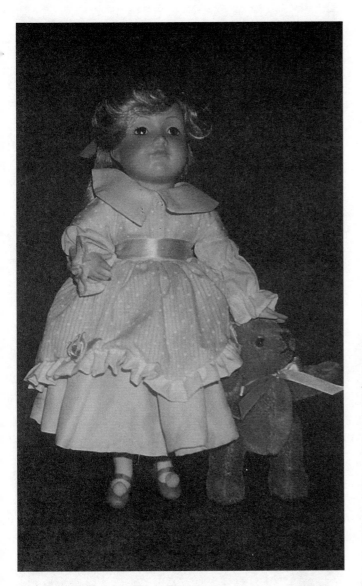

"Goldilocks" by Carol Lawson, 1984. Hand painted, pink dress, and dotted apron, white sleeves and collar. Painted shoes with pompoms. Franklin Mint. She has a teddy bear, which is another passion of the particular doll collector who owns her; $450-$550.

Reproduction of a French Fashion doll. Mohair wig, light blue eyes, bisque head, hands, and feet. Cloth body. Taffeta dress trimmed with old lace and hat, which boasts violets; 1985; $800-$850.

At left is a reproduction of a JDK Googly,
which is 9", bisque, and wears a pink satin
dress. Made by doll artist Donna Frame of
Concord, California; 1987; $250-$300. The
seated baby doll was made in Germany. It has
brown sleep eyes, open mouth, two teeth
MOA-150 Welsch-9 1/2". Value, $325-
$400.

"Goose Girl" by Jerri McCloud. Hand-painted
bisque porcelain fully jointed, brown glass eyes,
19th century dress. "Dolls by Jerri" label sewn
in dress seam. Porcelain goose is not shown.
She's wearing a Jerri McCloud club pin; 1988.
Value, $900-1,000.

Lee Middleton's "Little Angel Face," left, signed; 13". All vinyl, set glass blue eyes, blue dress, panties, and bonnet. White socks and shoes. Value, $550-$600. At right is Effanbee's "Baby Grumpy" reproduction, c. 1988. Reproduced in porcelain from the original composition version. "Limited Third Edition Doll Club" label sewn in garment. Head is engraved "Baby Grumpy LE"; $400-$500.

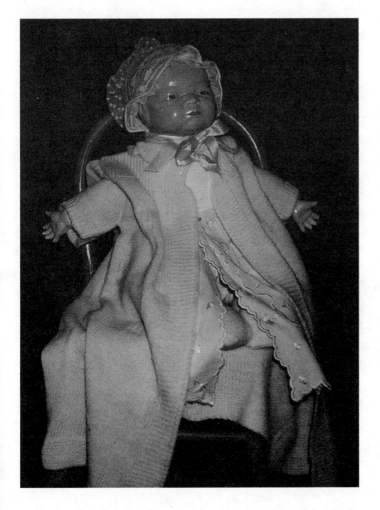

Composition Bye Lo, with cloth body and composition hands. Dressed in old baby clothes. Grace Putnam, 1923; $500-$550.

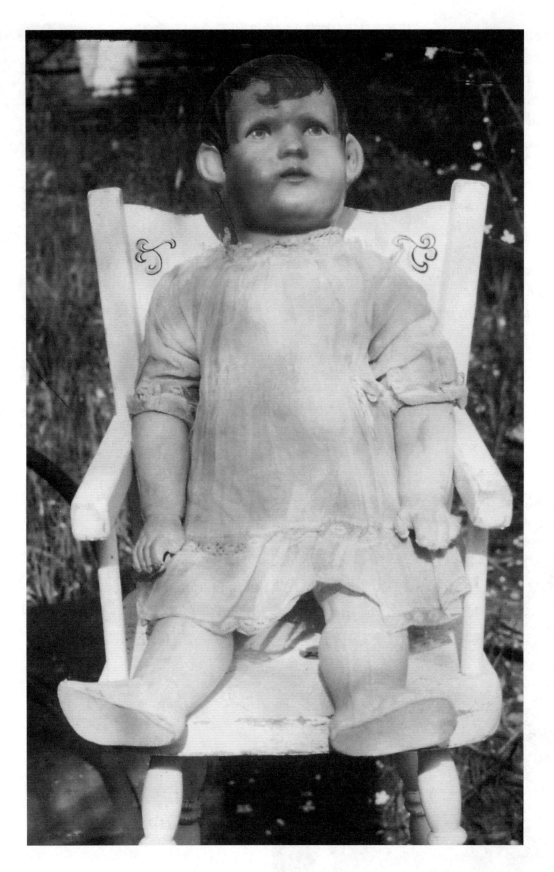

Completely papier mâché boy doll, not jointed or poseable, beautiful features, molded hair. Appraised, "as by an unknown maker 1920s." The owner has sought many opinions over a long period of time, but no one seems to recognize the maker. Possibly purchased in Europe in the late 1920s or early 1930s. An unusual doll and probably unique. Appraised in 1997 for $350.

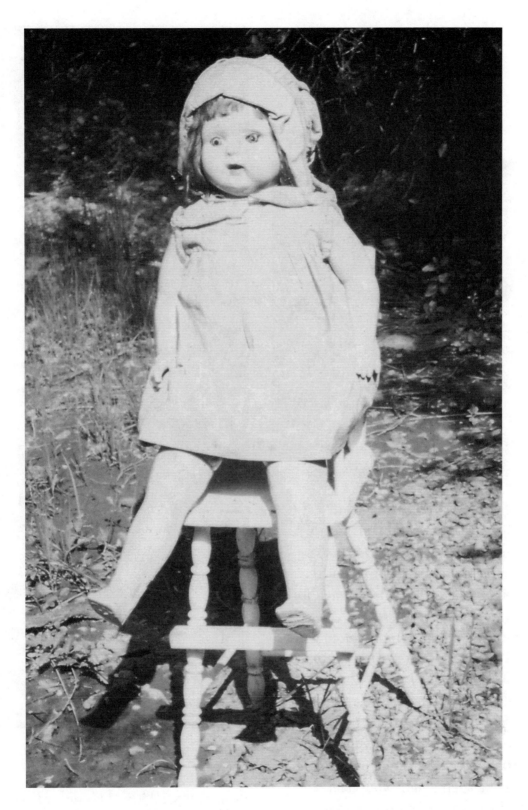

A large 1930s' doll, this is a good example of a typical doll of the mid-1930s. She was played with for a long time then put away and forgotten by the original owner. It has not seen the light of day for many years. The wig is a beautiful shade of auburn and she has bright blue eyes, which open and close. Original dress and cap are in a blue cotton print. Bought in the 1930s by the owner's grandmother, the owner remembers playing with her, probably the reason her socks and shoes are missing. In good , if not pristine, condition, she needs slight refurbishing. Too large for the 1940s' dolly high chair in which she sits. Valued by appraiser in 1997 at $175.

The Wives of Henry VIII, extravagantly costumed, 7" tall, perfect condition. Peggy Nisbit's first dolls were made in 1953 to commemorate the coronation of Queen Elizabeth of England and have long been noted for costume accuracy and detail. Nisbit's dolls were advertised in the Shannon Airport catalog (Ireland) in 1970 for $3.75 to $6 each, and in the Shannon 1976 catalog for $14.25 each. In 1986, Nisbit's Nell Gynne doll was selling for $29. Henry himself has always been somewhat more expensive. This price progression is so minor over such a period of time, one wonders how it could have been done. Now each wife has achieved 1998 status and is valued at $125-$175 on the secondary market.

This is "Puggy," who is irresistible. He is all composition and has molded and painted hair, as so many 1930s' dolls did. He is jointed, frowns adorably, and looks totally sly. Made by American Character, he dates from 1931 and his original owner still treasures him. The owner remembers playing with him as a young boy and called him "broder." This doll is "priceless" to the owner, but has been available on the market at around $400-$450.

This doll, Skookums, is made to resemble various tribes the owner feels represents the Taos, New Mexico area. It is an impressive example of this type of doll. These were made over a long period of time in various qualities, usually as inexpensive souvenirs. This is a better doll, dressed in original clothes; $150-$195.

This Rockford red-heel sock doll can trace its roots to early America. Think of the ingenuity of using a sock stuffed with whatever materials were available and then painting or drawing on a face, or as with this contemporary craft example, stitching appliquéd features. This one is stuffed with old nylon stockings and is already, at age 10, considered a family prize. Value, $45-$75.

In the doll world, life goes on for all the characters from "Gone With the Wind." Here are three unforgettable characters by World Doll. The tag reads, "Authentically crafted portrait dolls from the most popular film ever made." Value, $200-$300. This photo and the two following point to the wide-ranging choices we doll collectors have. The new doll artists often craft dolls in very different ways, as is evident in these pictures.

This fox terrier stood defense of an entire doll collection and made a handsome addition. He is collectible on his own. He is made of mohair, has a collar and very informative tag, which reads "FOX," and original "MARKE." In this condition, he should start at about $95, although I have seen examples selling for $125-$150.

Another Scarlett O'Hara and Rhett Butler
from World Doll. It is evident from all these
interpretations that dolls with the same basic
inspiration can and do take on very different
looks. Each doll is $250-$300.

Scarlett O'Hara and Rhett Butler, from the
Franklin Mint Heirloom Dolls Series, which
was authorized by MGM. These are bisque
porcelain and 19"; 2,000 were issued. Value is
$250-$300 for each doll.

Accessories

Accessories are becoming one of the most enticing aspects of the doll-collecting field–with or without the dolls. Small collectibles catching interest are the tin dishes, cups, saucers, pitchers, and tin tea sets of an earlier day.

The lithography is important here, as is condition, and as the field widens, the names of the manufacturers.

Today, avid adult collectors seek the tiny old tea sets and they are, indeed, adorable; the precious old hand-sewn clothing for their own dolls; and the doll "buggies" for displaying their own treasures or as a decorative item. How often have you seen just such a doll carriage resting in an elegant store window display?

Have you even seen a tiny leather coffin-shaped needle case replete with sterling silver needles, the hole so small the naked eye is hard put to encompass it? Probably not, because the rarities of the miniature world of dolls are disappearing so rapidly into collections it is a now-you-see-it, now-you-don't situation.

It is a commentary on these collectibles that collectors began because they loved the idea of these little unbreakable sets with the wonderful colors and designs and gave very little thought to who made them, but that has now become a very important factor in pricing.

These accessories, attractive and inexpensive back then, fit well into a doll setting and even the grandchildren could play with them (carefully).

Now that these little tin dishes have became so desirable, the prices have risen and the manufacturer's name becomes primary and will add to both buying and selling price. Do not let that influence you, however; some of the unmarked sets are the most endearing. Also, do not be timid about buying the odd saucer or cup, for just as in decorating your own home, you can use a colorful piece of this tinware to highlight a piece of doll furniture, or even a small no-so-bright corner of a collector's cabinet.

Many of these tiny accessories were made in Germany and France, but that has very little to do with quality; our home-grown varities are quite wonderful and you will be surprised if you have never considered tin dishes.

One American manufacturer of these

tiny treasures, the Ohio Art Company, prospered after World War I. Most European factories were left in disarray and imports to the United States all but ceased. Ohio Art had by then entered the toy field. The production of toy tinware did not begin until about 1920, after Ohio Art had acquired a large toy company. Names such as Chien and Amisco also were active in this market, but unless a piece is marked, it is difficult to tell who made what. Except in price it makes little difference: the old European pieces can be exciting, and many of them are unmarked.

Collectors should buy what interests them, whether it be theme, shape or color. Condition is important, however: just as you wouldn't spend money on a damaged doll unless the price was right and you couldn't live without her, the same principle applies here. Some collectors react positively to the occasional "character" dent or two–it's a personal decision.

If you collect or add to your doll collections with appropriate doll furniture, these tin-dish accents are a must, for with all their other attributes, they are unbreakable, surprisingly interesting, and very colorful.

Unbelievably tiny trunks to hold a fashion doll's luxurious necessities can also occasionally be found, and all of these very small wonders were supposedly to be set in trays for display in some very upscale salesroom of long ago. It must have been a veritable Aladdin's cave.

If the almost invisible small size doesn't interest you, doll-sized trunks might. We are probably likely to encounter those mostly from our own century and they can be incorporated into either a doll collection, as separate artifacts on their own, or as interesting storage for extra doll clothes. Bypass the tissue paper when packing extra costumes and use acid-free paper; also try to keep the little trunk, as well as your dolls, in a stable temperature.

These trunks come in a surprising number of coverings and materials. The metal trunks of the 1940s and '50s are most interesting when they have stickers, boast rather garish colors, or can be tied to a specific doll. The earlier trunks are still available, but often in poor condition. If you do not feel you have the skills to restore such a trunk, there are professional restorers; but bear in mind all such repairs today can be costly. The trunks are wonderful, though, and make a fascinating collection on their own

You cannot agonize over spending money for such treasures; there are too many collectors searching for them and accessories for the beautiful dolls have moved into a prime collecting position and are becoming more prominent at doll shows.

The French excelled at this sort of thing, and many of the smallest treasures were made to complement a fashion doll. No matter the origin, even newer miniatures–some by well-known artisans–are very popular.

Part of the motivation is space–we no longer live in huge rambling homes. Part of it is the fact that miniatures of all kinds have long been desirable to collectors and, in fact, have become a legitimate business by many craftsmen who market their diminutive art; part of it is the sheer attraction of these small treasures (can you easily resist that 1-inch pair of kid gloves?), with their precise measurements and attention to detail. It's a different aspect of doll collecting, but it all begins with the doll itself. These accessories merely accentuate the doll, although in fact some of them can be more expensive than the doll they highlight.

One of the great attributes of these accessories is that they put any doll in

This photo, taken in San Francisco c. 1914, illustrates the many different kinds of accessories available for dolls—from tiny washtubs and sewing machines to carriages, hammocks and dressers. If you collect or add to your doll collections with appropriate doll furniture, these items, along with tin-dish accents, are a must, for with all their other attributes, they are unbreakable and surprisingly interesting and very colorful. This photograph, by the way, is itself a collectible and was bought for $45.

Red and white tin dishes, stamped Ohio Art Co., Bryan., USA, and marked Bryan Q. USA; 1920s-1930s; $250-$350.

period–they define and place the doll in the correct time frame. Surrounded by the proper furniture, or extra clothing displayed on tiny period hangers, or the very small lorgnette or the diminutive kitchen utensils, adds validity and interest.

Take a leaf from a museum book and set your doll amidst a few accessories which define the period; it excites interest beyond the doll itself and explains without effort the years and events surrounding the time of the doll's popularity.

More painless but fascinating history, which while enlarging your doll collection and adding to your own knowledge, will certainly expand any other collector's awareness of history and nuances of the culture as well. It adds a whole new dimension to doll collecting–and it certainly makes it more interesting for anyone viewing such a display.

Since all of these little accessories are becoming choice and expensive, the collector should frequent the best and largest doll shows where more and more dealers are exhibiting them. It is a fun and educational way to exhibit your collection, but as prices rise you need to shop wisely and be sure your miniatures are in scale with your dolls.

Finding these Made in China copies of her Ohio Art Co. tin dishes was a shock to the collector. They are well done and who knows what the future will bring when the oval gold Made in China sticker has disappeared. This set features The Three Bears. The art work is good and the price is right if you don't mind owning a new set rather than the originals. The pieces of both these sets match the originals in both shape and number of pieces and are $20-$25.

All this accessory collecting is not new, but many of the current dolls–American Girls Collection for one–emphasize this aspect. Of course, in today's market, it is not essential to own the basic doll in order to collect the accessories.

An antique pressed wood dresser, 9-3/4" tall, 6" deep, and 12" wide. This lovely little dresser holds beautiful tin dishes marked "Made in France" and stamped "France." The round dish with children and horse is named by its owner "Horse Scene" and the plate is stamped U.S.A. Probably late 1890s, the dresser is $95-100.

A close up of the "horse-scene" plate and dishes marked "France." Set, $350-$400.

This is an excellent example of how to display your tin dishes in a natural sort of way. Sideboard is 22" tall, 12" wide, and 6" deep. Closed doors conceal other tin dishes, but visible on the shelves are blue tin dishes stamped "Germany."

The same sideboard as above, with doors open to reveal various other pieces of tin ware.

Close up of dishes on shelves of the side-board. A particularly desirable Christmas scene on plate. The birds on other dishes are very well done and are blue with touches of green.

A different bird scene is shown on this larger plate.

Here is still another example of imagination on display. The collector of these accessories is also a doll maker and her latest doll sits reading at her tea-table set with a vintage cloth and her tin cup of tea. The doll is cloth and hand painted, with hair that was put on her head one strand at a time. The teddy bear on the cup makes it a very lovable and collectible item. The cup and saucer are stamped "Germany." Value, $95-$120.

A washtub with small washboard. There is wonderful lithography on the good condition (slight edge chip) tub, which has a rather feminine pink interior. Marked with circle logo-J. Chein; c.1920s-30s; $250.

A 1930s' art-deco kitchen range. Small cooking utensils on the range itself are aluminum and from the 1950s-1960s. Value is $325-$375 without kettle, covered tiny pot, etc. These are also expensive now.

Collectors often have to buy these items one at a time, since the complete set is rarely found together, especially in this condition. Set, $375-$400. The lower shelf has a Japanese luster spice set which is also difficult to find; $295-$325. The doll-size coffee grinder is marked "Little Tot." The drawer also opens; $500-$550.

This carpet sweeper, with its beautiful colors and lithograph, is marked "Pretty Maid Toy Vacuum. Louis Marx and Co., Made in U.S.A." It measures 3-1/2" x 4". The brush is in good condition. This is one of a large collection of tiny sweepers. This type ranges from $65-$150.

The small wash-day helpers of bygone days are becoming scarce. The wringer, the tiny sewing machine, the wash-dayboiler, the dolly clothesline, the card of small clothespins marked "Clothespins and Line Set," (pins are colored)—all of these things which have been overlooked are now coming into their own. Prices will astonish you.

A closer view of the wringer and clothespins.

This pine dry sink is possibly a hand-crafted item. It is divided on the inside into two compartments, one for washing, one for drying. It is caulked so that it holds water and also has a removable cork so water can be let out. It's 12" high, 16-1/4" wide and 9-3/4" deep. The small-size wire-dish holder, positioned next to a small sized blanket/towel rack, is a very interesting item. Dry sink, $325-$395.

This black walnut table, with two extended sides, measures 14-1/2" long, 8" high, and 7-1/2" wide. Value, $175-$195.

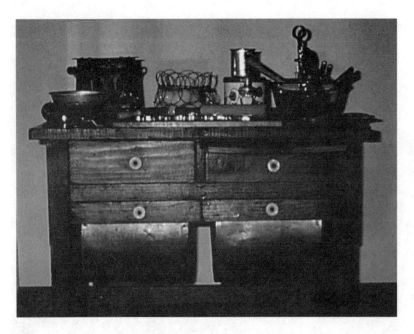

Double-bin table, pine with dark stain. Measures 15-1/4" high, 19-1/2" wide, and 11" deep. Wonderful piece of small furniture. Original condition; $550-$650. On the bin table are an electric toaster from the 1930s, which works well; a 1950s' aluminum colander, cookie cutters, various utensils, a child's wire egg basket holding pigeon nesting eggs, an embossed crumber set, a 1950s' salesman's sample Depression Glass salt and pepper shakers, and a wolverine strawberry Sunny Suzy Mixer set.

A child's dresser, oak. It measures 23" high, 15" wide, and 8" deep; c. 1890-1910. One knob has been replaced; $325-$375.

Pine dresser, painted white, floral trim, brass accents, mirror, same measurements as the oak dresser, c. 1890. On the dresser is a swirl candlestick, toothbrush holder from a dresser set, sugar bowl from a china set, Hull Pottery blank pitcher and bowl set from the 1960s, and a doll straw hat.

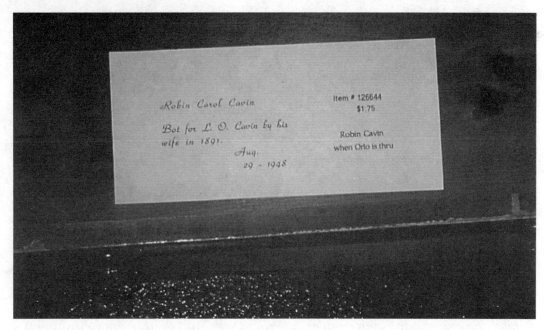

The following note was found inside the top drawer of the pine dresser: "ROBIN CAROL CAVIN BOT FOR L.O. CAVIN BY HIS WIFE IN 1891 ITEM 3126644 $1.75." Dated Aug. 29, 1948.

Child's oak sideboard with drawer, mirror, shelf, and double door closing on lower cabinet. It measures 13-1/2" high, 17" wide, and 8" deep; 1890-1910. Value, $375-$475. Also shown is an American Shield caster set, valued at $195-$210; glass candlesticks, and an old vintage doily, valued at $15-$20.

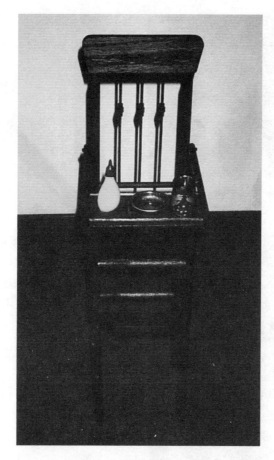

This doll high chair, made of oak, is another great accessory to a doll collection.

This Cass kitchen cabinet holds an array of dishes, bowls and other kitchen gadgets.

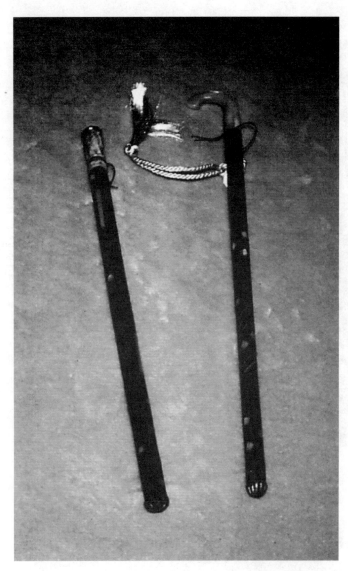

The walking sticks are each 9" long, and made of the finest materials. One has mother-of-pearl. This precious antique miniature is valued at $200-$300. The other also has mother-of-pearl, with topaz and amethyst stones, and a sterling silver bezel; $275-$350.

A sterling silver child-size curling iron; $185-$200.

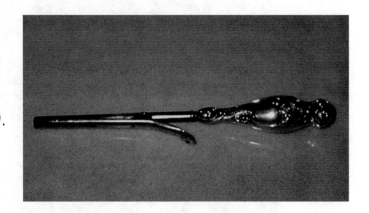

Other accessories collectors can sometimes find are unbelievably tiny trunks that hold a fashion doll's luxurious necessities.

We are probably likely to encounter those mostly from our own century and they can be incorporated into either a doll collection, as separate artifacts on their own, or as interesting storage for extra doll clothes. When packing extra costumes, use only acid-free paper and keep trunks and dolls in a stable temperature.

None of the small trunks featured in the collection on this page have maker's marks.

The trunk at left is cardboard on wood, metal trim and slightly domed; c. 1900. Often these older examples are found with broken latches or hinges. Price should definitely reflect overall condition, but keep your expectations reasonable and hope for a pleasant surprise. Children must have dearly loved these trunks, for rarely are they found in "un-played"-with condition as sometimes dolls are. Paper over wood, 12" x 7". Value, $300-$400. The newer trunk, top right, has travel stickers, which are a real plus. Australia, Hawaii, and France were not such commonplace destinations as they are now. The trunk itself is wood covered with paper, equipped to travel with a doll with hangers, and has one drawer. In "used" condition, but if resale is not involved, it is better to leave it as is since nothing important is missing or disastrously damaged. This trunk represents a steamer trunk in miniature. Paper over wood; 12" x 7". The owner remembers playing with this in the 1940s. Value, $50-$75. The slightly larger trunk is probably a child's. Victorian and all metal, with mustard-colored paint; original interior tray, with a Victorian picture. Refinished interior has paisley and is embossed with flowers. Measures 20" long and 12" high. Metal banding, all brass lock. Value, $350-$400.

Another doll trunk, embossed metal with original hardware, key, casters, leather handles, and original paint. Insert has original scrap. Measures 12" high, 10" deep and 18" wide; c. 1860s. Value, $500-$600.

The collector of these trunks positioned a 12" Ginny (Little Red Riding Hood) doll near the steamer trunk for size perspective.

114

Ethnic Dolls

The world keeps getting smaller and we all keep getting more sophisticated. Dolls, too. Ethnic dolls, both old and new, have become increasingly popular and perhaps that is why they begin to seem somewhat less exotic to our eyes. The Japanese Geisha figure, for example, is apt to be seen in almost any setting today–sometimes encased in glass, sometimes not; sometimes it is used purely as a decorating accessory. If you do not have a passion for dusting, you'll keep yours in a cabinet or its own glass case.

This kind of collection can be spectacular and exhibit dazzling color.

Where once a good, older Japanese doll would cost about $40 or $50, prices now can reach any heights. Some years ago, a West Coast department store exhibited a collection of male Japanese warriors, with prices, which then, seemed high but in retrospect seem rather moderate. That's the way the doll world has moved upward.

The Oriental dolls have always had a following. The fan base has increased considerably and while prices are still uneven because of the individuality of the dolls, almost all are moving into the mid to high hundreds of dollars.

Inexpensive airport type "Dolls of the World" have always been considered an unexceptionable souvenir, but this scene has changed somewhat. We now tend to bypass the inexpensive dolls of the countries we visit and think more in terms of well-known designers and company names from these far-away places. Serious collectors now look for dolls of great beauty and interest to add to collections. It is getting more exciting all the time and not at all unusual anymore.

Dolls of the World have always had believers, but those were not primarily bought based on artist or maker's name. Peggy Nisbit is an exception; her name on English dolls of kings, queens, and prime ministers was sufficient to promote her figures especially in England, but most collections of the earlier types bought while traveling were not of the quality of those available in today's market.

In the case of some of these dolls, often it is the costuming which will sell the doll, so Dolls of the World collections are bought primarily because of clothing they wear, which usually features typical garments of the foreign country we are visiting. There are some wonderful dolls being sold in this way now, so we can bypass, except as souvenirs, the usual inexpensive, small, and poorly made figures.

Again, any way you choose to express your interest in dolls, or in a foreign culture, is valid, but in any genre, always choose the best you can afford.

Dolls from other cultures now moving into our orbit is probably due to the rise of the fame of the artists themselves, as well as the well-promoted and attended big national and international doll shows. Then, too, home-shopping networks are helping publicize some of these wonderful dollmakers. The Internet is also becoming a factor.

Never lose contact with the burgeoning ethnic market. The doll world has gone from almost pristine white to a marvelous mix of colors and backgrounds. Where once a minority person had to look long and hard to find a good doll of color, the exercise is now made easy by the issue of ethnic dolls by all the major manufacturers.

This has occurred because of the demographics in this country, which show a fast-growing minority population which until lately has been largely ignored by doll makers. Of course, G. I. Joe was issued in a black version way back in 1965.

Matchbox Toys, Mattel, Little Tykes, the list of manufacturers now adding to the available list of dolls of color have realized the financial potential in this market, but there are other motives at work as well: some makers have realized the importance of dolls to growing children of every racial background, all of whom will have to learn to live together in harmony.

As usual, dolls have taken center stage in this learning process. As a tool for reflecting on life's vagaries, now, as through history, the doll has proved incomparable.

Alaskan dolls

Some of the finest examples of genuine American ethnic-doll art are produced in Alaska. At one time, you could certainly buy such dolls mostly in very specialized shops in the lower states or perhaps by mail; now you can also do so on the Internet–or better still, plan a cruise on the real Alaskan waters. You'll not only visit one of the most beautiful places on earth, you will be able to buy yourself one of the choice dolls made there.

The U.S. government sponsored a tour of such native arts some years ago, featuring desirable hand-crafted dolls, which were considered very unusual because of their marvelous clothing. Today, so many tourists are visiting our beautiful Northern neighbor and buying good dolls as souvenirs, more native Alaskan dolls are turning up in collections.

The arts and crafts of Alaska are promoted rather diligently and most artists sign their work, so collectors should always ask.

Lorena Hess of Anchorage is certainly an interesting dollmaker. Born in Mexico, she was transplanted to Alaska as an infant with her parents, who started a fur business. Her father taught her to stretch, cut, and sew fur, and when her brother was asked to make a doll by a visitor to Alaska, the doll business began.

Even from photographs, the quality of her doll clothing is evident, and the dolls themselves are outstanding examples of true native faces. These dolls represent an excellent way to build an ethnic collection: if possible, you should always try for a maker who is of a particular place and culture, rather than an interpretation by someone not rooted in that culture.

In the newest way of dollmaking, also used by her late brother Jose, Lorena uses resin for the faces, which are entirely hand-painted and then airbrushed. The ulu and spear are handcarved. Hess' daughter is now being trained in the dollmaking craft, Alaskan style.

What is really wonderful about these dolls is the never-to-be-forgotten facial expressions, and the unbelievable, sumptuous clothing.

The clothing represents the major influence of nature on the people of Alaska–the weather. Furs, beaded trim, and the typical hooded outer wear necessary in a frigid winter, make for very exotic doll costumes. Entire collections are now being assembled of Alaskan dolls by particular artists.

Be sure to acquire the provenance along with the doll, since this bodes to become a popular segment of doll collecting.

Hess also uses the Internet to market her dolls, which indicates life is getting simpler for us compulsive buyers.

Asian dolls

The Asian doll is making a huge impact. It is not a new collectible, but it is exotic and most collectors have interesting stories to tell about their Oriental dolls. One of the most intriguing of all doll stories of any genre has to do with the Friendship Dolls of Japan.

The report begins just the way a fairy tale might: "Early in 1927, a great number of specially treated passengers were on two steamers bound for Japan, one from New York and one from San Francisco. They were more than 12,700 little dolls and each of them carried her own passport and visa. Each doll carried a message for Japanese children which read, 'This doll is a good citizen of the United States of America. She will obey all the laws and customs of your country. Please take care of her while she is with you...I am being sent to Japan on a mission of friendship. Please let me join the Girls' Festival in your country."

Farewell parties were held when the dolls set out amid much festivity.

This unique cargo was part of a Doll Mission of Friendship, an attempt to stem anti-Japanese feeling in the United States in connection with the war. In Japan, where most children had never seen an American doll, these were eagerly awaited. When they arrived in Yokohama, welcome parties were held and the dolls were given to nearly every school. "The children were struck with wonder," the report says, and "impressed with the doll's blue eyes."

Japan decided to return the favor and 58 dolls were made and one or two was sent to each major city in the United States. These were called "Dolls of Gratitude" and when they landed in San Francisco, they were given a warm welcome. Berkeley, Oakland, Chicago, and New York also received dolls. These were then exhibited and placed in local museums or galleries.

In December 1941, after war had erupted, Japan's educational system fostered animosity against America. Thus, most of the precious dolls made by Americans and sent in friendship were destroyed.

The story reads like a master mystery: some teachers in Japan resisted the wanton destruction and hid the dolls, and it was not until years later they were discovered and put on exhibition.

More than 80,000 people viewed an exhibit of some rediscovered "Dolls with Blue Eyes" and "Dolls of Gratitude." Some required restoration and new kimonos, but everywhere they went, tremendous

Contemporary doll makers of these types of dolls are so few, they are almost non-existent. No firm secondary market prices have been established for the new Asian doll artisans. Most dolls are crafted to order in such limited supply, they are often acquired immediately by museums. Since these dolls are custom made, prices are set by the doll maker. Custom-made dolls by Kazuko Tamaoki, who crafts Oyama-style dolls, are of such beauty collectors eagerly add her limited output to their collections. Rosie Skiles, one such collector, says Tamaoki is a "master of her art, and also is a skilled restorer of old Japanese dolls, which brings tattered faded dolls to new life." This information is important to collectors of these old dolls, since such restoration is a very rare skill.

This 24" Ichimatsu bends in three places and has a lovely silk-crepe fan design. The doll was created to resemble Kazuko Tamaoki's daughter, Yoko, when she was young; it actually has her daughter's human hair. Value, $6,000-$7,000.

excitement was generated.

Japanese American Doll Enthusiasts, a very active organization, tracks all these dolls and conducts an on-going search for 16 still missing. A gala reunion of the dolls is planned for the year 2002.

This poignant story highlights the value dolls have on many levels aside from pleasure and profit. Think back to childhood–did dolls you owned (or dolls you did not) affect you in any way? An anecdote related in a seminar I was teaching is apropos: "You know," said a middle-aged participant, "I've just realized why I love and collect Japanese fans. My father served in the Korean war and when he came home, he brought me a Korean doll and she carried a lovely fan. I still have the doll, but lost the fan. I guess at heart I'm still looking for it."

Many large Asian doll collections continue to be made, not only from Japan and China, but from Korea, Indonesia, Thailand and other unusual places, and individual artisans are adding their wonderful hand-crafted skills to this field. Some of these newer examples are now in museums and considered genuine fine art.

Since the entire world is becoming more accessible to all, including the doll collector, the field has become more general and international dolls are regularly entering the lists of popular collectibles. This is not only interesting but, as with the Japanese Friendship Dolls, tends to promote a feeling of crossing cultural barriers. It opens new windows on the world, a new perspective on history. We see typical costumes of the country, some of them newly made but evocative of the past; we see different facial expressions, different features, coiffures, even traditional characteristic poses of a particular place. We also see different materials used to clothe the dolls and a different base for the faces which does not crack.

New doll artisans such as W. Harry Presyk of Sacramento, Calif., are a part of this enlarging scene and contribute greatly to this field, not only with specific skills, but with decided originality.

The dolls of Japan are the largest segment of this field, which have been, in many cases, meant to be treasured heirlooms given to girls at birth and brought out once or twice a year during the "Girl's Festival" to be exhibited, admired, and then carefully put away until the next grand occasion. These dolls can vary greatly in size (some are tiny), but their costumes speak essentially of Japan, its customs, and its working people. Even these vary from simple to ornate.

The coveted so-called "egg shell" faces on some older dolls were made of oyster shell, which was powdered, mixed with glue, and then polished. These dolls tend to bring a higher price and add to the rather mystic feeling some of these figures project. In fact, many Japanese dolls were not really considered dolls in the sense we mean; they were "figures" constructed and costumed in the images of great warriors, the sensuous Geisha, even great personages of Japan. The word doll itself translates to approximately "human figure."

There are wide choices here, from easily recognized figures such as the Hakata type, which were crafted to represent people doing everyday things–selling pots and pans, fish, or bakery goods–to the elegantly clad ceremonial figures. Whether the garb is elegant or humble, almost all dolls are costumed correctly and with fine materials.

One of the most familiar dolls is the "Maiden with Hats," or, as some people call her, "the Hat Seller." Technically, she is a "sakuro"–ningyo–we usually call her one of the cherry dolls. She is actually performing the "Dance of the Seven Hats," which interprets a classic Japanese folk tale. The hats are usually silk and basically she is formed over a wire frame. This is a fairly familiar doll to us. We've seen it often, probably because cherry dolls are now being produced in large commercial numbers for export. This fact points up the increasing popularity of this field of collecting.

If a diligent collector manages to assemble a goodly number of Japanese dolls, it might be said it is an "impact collection." It will be stunning, vivid with color, and diverse even within the one collection.

Here is an area of collecting which was neglected for a long time, and great bargains could have been had, but now recognition for these dolls has soared in this country and prices keep rising. This type of doll requires a certain kind of appreciation of the culture and background of the figure to be fully understood, but on any level, they are interesting and worthwhile.

Irish dolls

The Crolly dolls of Ireland are as exquisite as Fiannuala or as fascinating as Padraig, the net mender. As with the wonderful Irish Belleed, with its many patterns evocative of the sea, these character dolls of Crolly are taken from the experience of the long Irish culture itself.

They are carefully and meticulously crafted and appropriately and admirably costumed. Even at Dublin Airport, where one would expect to find, as in "olden days," lesser-quality dolls for sale, these high-quality figures sell for surprisingly fair prices. The dolls are quite beautiful and in Ireland there is a great demand for them; in fact, at Christmas time, queues at stores across Ireland are the norm, with one or two dolls the limit per customer.

Mostly unknown in the United States, this is a market all doll lovers should be aware of. The history of the company is interesting. Its beginnings in 1939 in an old factory building in Crolly, County Donegal, were with small dolls having composite head, hands, and feet, soft-filled bodies, and dressed in clothing made with local fabrics and hand-knitted garments.

In the early 1950s, Crolly began experimenting with vinyl paste with great success; thus, the molding and production of plastic play dolls "went into full swing."

All the dolls are produced from original sculptures, which are now hand crafted by an in-house designer and sculptress identified by the company only as "Claire." In the rather modest, endearing Irish way (certainly unusual today), all the important people involved in the production of these beautiful dolls are designated in the same unassuming manner–by first names only.

Crolly, in fact, is the only doll maker in Ireland which does its own sculpting, makes its own molds and porcelain slip, and "dresses the dolls in the finest of Irish fabrics, hand-woven Donegal tweeds, Irish linens, etc." Who could possibly ask for more in any one doll? In fact, it is unusual today to have a doll made entirely in one place–from design inspiration to fully dressed figure.

An unusual new direction for this company is the release of a collection of miniature porcelain 18th- and 19th-century hats. Utterly marvelous., and engagingly called Pipkin & Bonnet, each meticulously crafted and exquisitely executed headpiece is accompanied by its own tiny hat box. This will certainly make a stunning accessory for any doll display.

One of the most appealing facets of Crolly dolls is the excellence of the molded faces and figures; the faces are not all the same and the figures representing various types of people in various types of

Sculpting the head of Padraig.

The Crolly dolls of Ireland are beginning to attract accolades in the American market for their beauty and craftsmanship. The fact that they are made entirely by hand in one location, Ireland, is most unusual today and permits stringent quality control, which assures the integrity of each doll. Not only are the Colleens stylish, charming, and gracefully costumed, but the character dolls crafted by this talented group are fascinating. (More Crolly dolls are featured on pages 135-136.)

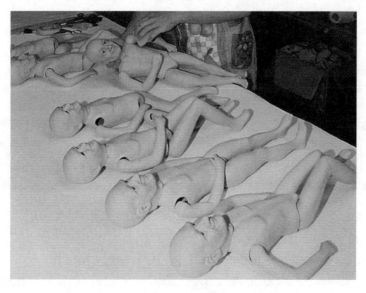

Dolls at the stringing stage.

Jan McLean of New Zealand is a prime example of an artist whose work is being recognized as exceptional and memorable. She is a master of facial expression and her dolls are finding an eager market. Her hand-made ceramic dolls are considered genuinely fine art by discerning collectors world wide. Prices range from $2,000 to $12,000, although no firm secondary market prices have been established, probably because collectors have not been persuaded to part with these very limited-edition dolls. Karma, shown here, is a limited-edition series of 100. Made of porcelain, she has an exquisite face and her costume is magnificent and thoroughly eye-catching.

crafts are amazing.

The company says that creating and manufacturing these dolls in the unspoiled west of Ireland is responsible for the continued inspiration for the delicacy and astounding beauty and charm of Crolly dolls. It may very well be true. If you have ever been in western Ireland and stood quietly on that rather supernatural misty shore, you could well imagine a gorgeous auburn-tressed mermaid stopping by to say hello—no doubt Crolly and Miss Claire feel this, too.

New Zealand dolls

We are accustomed to great doll art and fine dolls from Europe, Germany, and France, so it is exciting to contemplate the widening of the doll production on such a high scale from countries we have not before considered the bastions of great art, even though they may have backgrounds of excellent dolls with which we have not been familiar—Ireland, New Zealand, and Thailand are just a few of these which now must be considered in this enlarging new world of ours.

New Zealand is a crafts-oriented country so it is not too surprising to find its doll artists and makers achieving a strong place in the doll world. Even a small city such as Dunedin in the south boasts many working doll artists. If you have a strong interest in the dolls of this country, the big, well advertised doll shows, in New York for example, are your best opportunity.

At that show, you may very well meet doll artist Jan McLean of "Jan McLean Originals, Collectible Designer Dolls." This artist and her dolls are fast-rising stars in the doll heavens. One of the characteristics of her creations are facial expressions which lend all her dolls a very alluring, yet somehow innocent, charm.

In a relatively few years, she has moved from a home-based business to an enterprise which now employs nine people working in her "studio," plus a retail outlet and gallery, and all of it keeps expanding.

Her dolls have achieved world-wide acceptance since her first appearance at the New York Doll show and her limited-edition porcelain beauties command high prices and high priority for collectors. The "limited" edition means just that, some are in the 100-production figure, but as the world moves, so does McLean. And so the expensive, very limited-edition dolls are giving way to more mass-production dolls.

While porcelain has always been a favored material for dolls, it is not easy to obtain in New Zealand, so McLean has turned to resin—and the results are startling in their natural look. This maker feels resin is a big part of the doll-making future, and her dolls, with their exquisite faces and elaborate costumes, will prove she is no doubt correct.

Here again is an artist who says she inherited her skills and artistry from her mother and grandmother; she is that raris avis: artistic and highly creative and also a fine businesswoman—all at the same time.

She is about to expand into Europe and as this maker widens her world, be sure to look for one of those 100-edition originals. And keep an eye on the resin dolls, which are an example of her purveyance of great beauty and wondrous elegance.

Sue Todd is another doll artist from Dunedin.

Her doll window displays in a local shop are really eye catching, and the dolls are beautifully dressed and reasonably priced for their quality.

Other discoveries

It is well for serious collectors to

become aware of the new avenues in the search for beautiful, well made, and costumed dolls. Some names have not yet surfaced in the United States as premier doll makers, some are slowly gaining recognition, and many are on track to become famous for their production of small-edition, highly desirable collectible dolls. Collectors who want to widen their interests should try to attend an international doll show if at all possible; if not, target one of the big national toy or doll shows as your annual vacation destination. You will be amazed at what is out there that is still unfamiliar to us.

What a prospect—an exciting vacation jaunt to see fabulous dolls. A real advantage to doing this is the possibility of acquiring a precious doll which has not yet achieved complete recognition, whose designer is still somewhat unknown. A dedicated collector never feels limited—intelligent collecting calls for awareness of all possibilities.

Consider the highly exotic dolls of Indonesia. As many more people are visiting that country, travelers are adding some beautiful Indonesian dolls to collections. So far, these have made inroads primarily into Asian-doll collections and collections of Dolls of the World, but the best of them are beginning to stand on their own—and often on ornate magnificent doll stands—and new collections are being born.

Try Alaska. If you have had the advantage of visiting one of the most truly magnificent places on earth, you may have bought yourself a souvenir doll. As always, it was hopefully a finer example of the many for sale and hopefully, too, it started you on a new tangent in dolls.

This interesting 10" wooden doll of the Tutiyu strain was made by Honda Hiroshi, 1934. Value, $500-$600.

124

Extremely elegant, this doll is dressed in a silk kimono and carries a lantern. The owner always refers to this figure as the "Lady of the Night." As with all others in this collection, she is kept in an individual framed case. Value, $195-$250.

The work of a clever, imaginative Asian-doll artisan from Sacramento, California, W. Harry Perzyk, is absolutely stunning. The dolls on the next four pages are all his original copies.

Yoshimobu, pictured here, is a Japanese warrior of the 16th-17th century and made of porcelain. Value, $3,000-$3,500.

This wood carving of Hideyoshi Toyotomi, a Japanese warrior of the 16th-17th century, has a value of $9,000-$10,000.

Yoritomo, made of porcelain, is a 16th-17th century Japanese warrior. Value, $3,000-$3,500.

"Gatutkaca," an Indonesian doll, is made of porcelain. Value, $1,250-$1,500.

Kagetora, a Japanese warrior from the 16th-17th century, is made of porcelain and valued between $3,000-$3,500.

Murasaki, a geisha, is made of porcelain.
Value, $850-$1,000.

A contemporary solid-wood carving, this cave
man has a value between $2,250-$2,500.

The dolls on this page, a collection of older Asian dolls, with their glowing costumes and intricate, innocent-looking seductive poses, are a stunning sight. Older Japanese dolls will inevitably cost more on the secondary market.

Washi is a 10" male paper doll made in Japan. These dolls typically do not have facial features. Value, $50-$100.

This warrior riding on a white horse—the detail of the armor is striking—is used on Boys Day for display. Value, $700-$800.

WANTED

Help is needed to find sixteen missing, priceless friendship dolls.

MISS CHIBA

MISS TOKYO-FU

MISS NIIGATA

MISS NAGANO

If you have information about these any of these friendship dolls, please write or call:

Rosie Skiles
718 Bunting Drive
Lafayette, CO 80026
Phone (303) 665-9767

Japanese **A**merican **D**oll **E**nthusiasts

Although the 58 Ambassadors of Friendship sent from Japan are not all identical, they all have characteristics in common. Certain criteria must be met, or the doll will be ruled out as a possibility. These dolls were made to represent a six year old girl with a bob hair cut. The doll must be 32" (81 cm) tall, and of the ichimatsu type (meaning it can bend at the hip, knee and ankle). The skin is of gofun which looks like egg shell but made of ground oyster shell and glue. They have glass inset eyes. Some dolls have open mouths showing teeth, and others have closed mouths. The faces reflect the style of each individual craftsman, with subtle differences in fullness of cheeks, and in expressions. The color and design of the original kimono vary but they were made of the finest silk chirimen crepe with a brocade obi . Accoutrements for the dolls are different but did include parasols, miniature black lacquered furniture and may include a stand, and letters from the prefecture from where it came.

Japanese American Doll Enthusiasts has distributed this poster in the hopes of tracking down Miss Yokohama's sister dolls, all of whom are considered "priceless." If one should ever be discovered on the secondary market, contact the museum or Rosie Skiles.

Thai dancers, an overlooked segment of the doll world, wear very ornate costumes. They are all cloth over wire armature and have painted features. Value depends, to some extent, on costume, $35-$45.

This Japanese lady represents "Kakata Ning Yo," a character from a well-known drama. She is holding a warrior's head piece in her hand. Constructed of cloth over wire armature, her silk-covered face and feet are beautifully painted. Value, $145-$200.

This Oyama doll, made by Kazuko Tamaoki, has a gofun face and wears a lovely black-silk kimono, with ocean waves on the hem. The doll is 18" and custom made. Value, $300-$500.

This male doll, Mrs. Tamaoki's newest creation, was custom made. Value, $3,000-$4,000.

Kazuko Tamaoki often places her dolls within a scene, such as these two ladies visiting and kneeling beside a floral arrangement. This would be considered a formal call. Value, $3,000-$4,000.

Another Jan McLean original, Delphine, a
limited edition of 100, is made of porcelain.
Notice the differences in expression in Karma
and this doll, the wonderful craftsmanship of
the hands, and the fabulous costume.

Rose is a limited edition of 250. This doll is
resin, an entirely new concept. Jan McLean
began experimenting with this material about
18 months ago when she realized its potential.
This beautiful doll is thus a pioneer in the world
of dolls, as is her creator.

The dolls on this page and the following one are more examples of Crolly dolls. The two character dolls, here, "Tom" and "Mary," are full porcelain and 22" tall. Each are valued between $225-$250.

Dolls sold at Dublin airport, 1997. The male doll at left is $129.95 and the female one is $99.95. These seem extraordinarily popular among European tourists. Prices on the U.S. secondary market, if indeed the dolls can be found, are $195-$250.

This delightful 17" "dancing doll" is named Cailin. She is made of porcelain and is on a wooden stand. Value, $175-$225.

Fionuala is made of porcelain. Her name is pronounced "Finn-oo-la" and she retails for under $200. A beautiful doll.

These Alaskan dolls by Lorena Hess are outstanding examples of true native faces. The clothing represents the major influence weather has on the people of Alaska. Furs, beaded trim, and the typical hooded outer wear, necessary in a frigid winter, make for rather exotic doll costumes. The spears are also handcarved.

A male doll with spear.

This female doll, with hand-beaded necklace, also carries an ulu knife.

French Fashion Dolls

You can accept it as a given that French fashion dolls are almost always exquisite in form, face, and dress; that they are scarce and expensive; that they are, for the most part, genuine antiques.

You will also be totally entranced with the accessories which often accompanied these dolls: the small trunks, the walking sticks, the parasols, the tiny jewelry. You will also need to have inherited Aunt Henrietta's fortune if you want to own one and if prices keep rising.

Of course, before the fashion plate became a more efficient tool for providing customers with visual aids to choosing a wardrobe, societies had used figures to demonstrate fashions to wealthy patrons. Royalty regularly ordered figures dressed to court standards for themselves and for shipment to other royal personages.

In Paris, outdoor stalls featured such dolls at least since the mid-18th century, dressed lavishly in costumes that if found in their original state, can accurately date a doll. It also adds to the cost. It is not unheard of to come upon such a treasure as an all-original French-fashion doll, although as the field becomes more attractive to collectors and museums covet these dolls, it gets more difficult.

There is evidence that these figures were sometimes shipped great distances to promote the fashions of a particular country or couturier, but once pictures in the form of etchings or plates were available in the late-18th century, the doll became superfluous as a demonstration selling tool. They had been in use for a long time, though, and even after the plates were widely used, fashion dolls were still being shipped to points around the world; so they didn't just disappear—they passed from the scene rather slowly.

Also, it is well to remember that during their time period, many shops were busy making these figures, as well as their accessories. The types of these dolls were countless and of different sizes and materials, so the bodies can be remarkably varied.

The costumes were purposely magnificent and ultra-feminine in order to promote French silks, satins, and laces; 18th-century French chic on a beautiful small figure—what could be more enticing?

The collector of these lovely dolls will own not only an elegant artifact, but a fascinating piece of history. The wise collector will take the time to study and learn; these dolls can teach history, politics and intrigue, as well as costuming and tailoring we can only envy today.

Some of the costumes were hand-made and some of the later ones were crafted by machine, but no matter. The materials–laces, furs, feathers, jewels–are all almost unbelievable and have to be studied to be appreciated.

Keep thinking about French fashion dolls, but pull your mind forward to the 1940s. World War II was over, the French economy was more than depressed, and the fashion industry was in a quandary as to how to resurrect Paris as the world fashion leader.

Brainstorming probably did it–some genius thought of the long-ago fashion dolls.

Thus, it was that the famous designers, with the backing of the entire couture industry with its best creative minds, and in collaboration with well-known theater artisans, decided to showcase French fashion on a well-designed set featuring superb small dolls–200 of them. These up-to-the minute mannequins would be displayed in magnificent theater sets. An inspiration.

Truly masterful designers did the clothing, great theater artistes designed the sets in which they were displayed, and the French government designed an exhibition program. The scope of the involvement of various skilled artisans seems almost unbelievable. Jewelers, shoemakers, hairdressers, dressmakers of every kind of clothing, and milliners all contributed to the marvel that was the "Théâtre De La Mode"–all for the glory of French couture. The idea and its execution were a huge success.

If ever we needed proof that even in the doll world things are cyclical, this unique collection is proof positive. It was made in 1945, it succeeded beyond dreams, and then it disappeared.

What happened to this wonderful piece of fantasy? Exact details are sketchy. It toured to great acclaim, appeared at the De young Museum, and the I Magnin and City of Paris department stores in San Francisco in 1946; from there its history is obscured.

It had been stored in San Francisco at the City of Paris until it was shipped to Maryhill Museum of Art in Washington state in the 1950s.

Alas, incredibly detailed and impressive theater sets were destroyed. Then nothing. There was a complete hiatus of these dolls.

Not until the 1980s did they resurface. The entire collection was uncovered in the United States at Maryhill Museum in Goldendale, Washington–itself a place of fantasy.

Now the future of Théâtre de la Mode is bright. Sent back to Paris in 1990, all the dolls were beautifully and accurately restored. The sets, too, have been rebuilt, and can now be seen again in all their glory. The entire collection has toured all the major cities of the world to great enthusiasm.

This collection has such impact, not only visually, but in its historic implications that doll collectors can only feel proud of its rediscovery and know that probably their interest helped promote its restored popularity.

So the fashion dolls of 1945-46 have helped focus attention on the earlier dolls of French fashion. The 1940s' Mannequins of Maryhill have a secure, beautiful home in Goldendale, while the older examples of fashion dolls are appearing in doll shows and collections with increasing regularity.

Interest is beginning to peak in all manner of Fashion dolls. It seems almost heavensent that all doll collectors can now view, if not buy, this historic Maryhill aspect of the Fashion doll and it is equally provident that for whatever reasons, a surprising number of these magnificent old French fashion dolls are available.

At a recent doll show, I counted 30 examples of these dolls, some quite extravagant. Naturally, not all have their original clothing or marvelous accessories, but some do. And when you find one you love with her dashing little reticule or ruffled parasol, think very carefully before you pass her by. She will be a joy forever.

This is a close-up view of one of the dolls pictured in the Paris Sketch on page 145. Mad Carpentier, dress and jacket ensemble, white (synthetic) linen waist-length blouson, two ceramic buttons. A deep fold from the waist forms extended shoulders. Full sleeves with gussets. Navy and white chevron pattern (synthetic) linen skirt. White artificial straw hat, linen crown trimmed with white moiré bow: Albouy. Coiffure: Guillaume. Beige leather sandals with navy blue heels: Maniatis. Navy suede gloves. Décor: Jean Saint-Martin.

Le Théâtre. Originally created by Christian Berard, the current re-creation is by Anne Surgers.

Street Scene from Théâtre de la Mode. The original stage set was designed in 1946 by Georges Wakhevitch.

The Rue le la Paix and Place Vendôme. Originally created by Louis Touchaques, the current re-creation is by Anne Surgers.

The Paris Sketch. Original stage set designed in 1945 by Jean Saint-Martin.

G.I. Joe

Maybe nostalgia for a lost past, even a contentious one, is part of the revived collectibility of G.I. Joe–the boy toy of the 1960s. As that generation matures, G.I. Joe represents childhood to many and since Joe was indeed intended as a plaything, he no doubt recalls happy moments.

Controversy swirled around Joe and his fellows: he represented violence, some claimed; he glorified war, said others; but somehow he survived wars, even retirement in 1978, and is now the subject of books, vast collections, and revived interest.

He was not too tall (12 inches), but tall enough; he was handsome; his physique was marvelous; he represented the Army, the Navy, and any branch of military service you thought about. He was really an "action figure," capable of feats of derring-do. He sported a dashing scar. He was a hero.

Hasbro, which made these moveable, jointed plastic figures, claims sales figures in the billions based on 220 million of the toys sold. The claim was that 60 percent of all American boys in the 1960s and '70s owned a G.I. Joe. Amazingly, the foreign market for Joe was also large (about 20 percent) and he was popular in Britain, France, and even Spain. He has been one of the most successful toys ever made.

Each figure sported a different shade of hair, even an unexpected redhead. The painted molded hair on the earlier figures gives them a totally different look. The reissued Joes are smaller and have a different appearance from the originals of 1964.

G.I. Joe did not travel light; he had changes of uniforms, extra pistols, rifles, helmets, boots, and a wonderful wooden military trunk, replete with rope handles with clearly marked spaces for name, rank, and serial number. It was a meticulously researched and manufactured toy.

Looking back, most collectors probably do not realize how popular Joe really was, but interest has revived and in 1998, Hasbro Toys issued a commemorative-figure Masterpiece Edition of G.I. Joe, which retails for $50. Only with this new edition can you acquire a booklet detailing all you want to know about "America's Greatest Fighting Man."

This plastic "action figure" was

unusually well jointed and pliable. His ability to bend, flick his wrists, and get easily into a "crawl" position indicates the care taken with details of his manufacture. The original was sturdy and survived hard play over long periods of time.

As with most of the 1960s' toys, poor Joe languished in many a thrift shop in the 1970s, but those who bought him at low prices, or kept him originally, can now glory in their good sense. G.I. Joe survived the Vietnam mentality and Desert Storm and is once again a hero, although any serious mention of war and world conflict is being downplayed.

Hasbro has been careful about describing the new G.I. Joe as an "adventurer" rather than "a fighting man," and although collectors of the original figures are not too thrilled by this new Joe or his escapades, they are happy to see him back in any sort of action.

The values of the 1960s' figures have risen dramatically. It was indeed a well-made toy and controversy or no, boys, for the most part, loved him. I know several serious collectors of G.I. Joe and his friends–some began with the dolls they owned as children–and not one seems to be pro-war or prone to violence. This makes for an enlivening evening's discussion.

Psychology not withstanding, look for Joe, and especially for his accessories, which are more difficult to find in good condition.

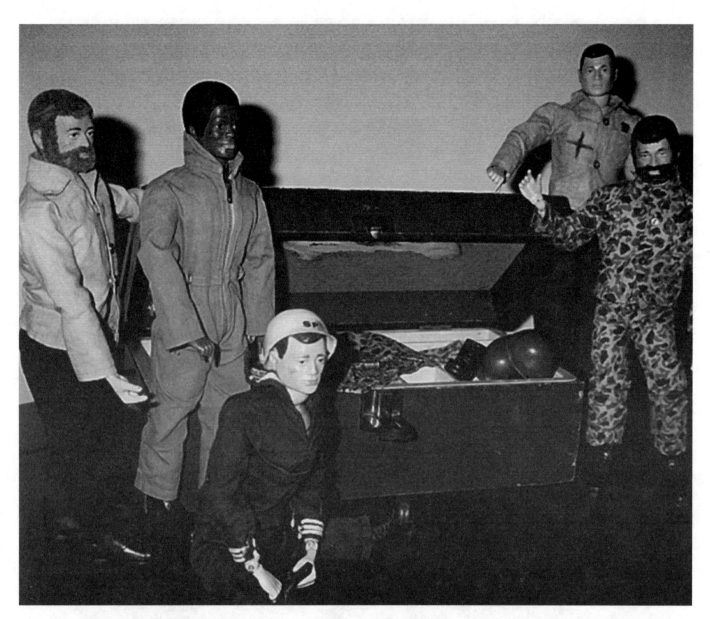

This photograph illustrates the wonderful construction of the basic G.I. Joe figures–they are easily posed in realistic ways, are handsome, and, as actual experience proves, almost indestructible. The costumes are accurate, the faces quite wonderful, and the diversity of the services represented shows excellent attention to detail. Notice the differences in the hair on some of the men. In these figures, the designer has created very life-like looking servicemen who seem to exude energy. The ability to bend them easily into a great variety of poses made for hours of happy playtime. The five figures here are originals from the 1960s and were strictly playthings, which endured very heavy use for some years. Happily, they were saved (almost accidentally) and are in excellent condition for all that. Their locker is also intact and holds an incomplete extra wardrobe. The names are inspired: "Adventure Team," the red-headed "Sea Adventurer," the "Black Avenger," and descriptions such as "Man of Action" and "Talking Soldier" were all guaranteed to appeal to active boys. Prices are surprising, since for many years there was little demand for Joe and his fellows, but price-guide prices are now beginning to dictate the market. Value, original figures, 1964 set with original box, $300-$350. Black G.I. Joe, 1965; value, $125-$150. This figure can also be found in collections of Black Memorabilia. Accessories, variable, range from $30-$125. All prices in this area are changing rapidly due to increased interest.

Modern Dolls and Artists

Artist-designed dolls are a big segment of today's doll market. The collector has wide choices, the variety is almost endless, and everyone agrees that the talents of the contemporary designers are monumental. As a matter of fact, as one collector asks in awe, "Have there always been so many marvelous doll artists around?"

Part of the success of these many talented people is the burgeoning doll market itself. So many collectors with such diverse tastes require enough people to craft enough beautiful dolls to satisfy the insatiable quest for beauty of face and costume. That quest is never ending, of course, since beauty is indeed in the eye of the beholder, so doll production has enlarged both in size and scope.

The series doll has also become so popular, it is difficult to keep up with the market. Among the makers, Goebel North America has produced dolls that are not only well crafted, but beautifully designed. It is a thoroughly consistent company and an excellent example of the recognition the larger makers are giving the unsung heroes and heroines—the artists.

At last doll designers have assumed a major role in the creation and costuming of dolls. The designers are now recognized as being important in their own right, a tremendous factor in the success of the newer dolls. Their name recognition alone can sell dolls.

The well-known couturiers have also achieved more fame on this smaller stage.

Barbie, for example, has worn fabulous clothes created by famous names in the fashion field. But long before Barbie, there was the fashion doll, and more recently, Madame Alexander, who in the early 1920s was dressing her dolls in the most imaginative way in beautifully made clothing.

A comprehensive collection of the still popular Nancy Ann dolls also points up the part costume has played in doll collecting. Nancy Ann, with her appealing, winsome face, is a study in costuming, with hundreds of dolls dressed in the most dainty, feminine way. It's truly an almost astonishing sight to see hundreds of these dolls, each dressed differently and each so lovely it is easy to take for granted the many talents employed. We so often do not consider the thought and work which went into it all.

Taken one at a time, it seems possible; taken as a whole, it seems impossible. This is the lure of a full collection—the appreciation of the collective beauty both of the doll itself and her costumes. Any doll, any costumes. It has to be seen en masse to be fully appreciated. Not that one doll is trifling, not so; but viewed as a whole, any doll collection has to be more interesting and gives us a better understanding of the basic collectible.

Shirley Temple dolls reflected the children's fashions of her time, all of them well designed and executed—so well done that even though many were designed for her films, the clothing is timeless and a wonderful example of good design. Her doll likenesses are also good examples of the role clothing has played in the promotion and selling of dolls through the years. Now there are many collectors seeking not only extra outfits for their own dolls, but some who collect only doll clothing—without owning any dolls.

The creators of the long ago French fashion dolls knew a thing or two about merchandising and while they were essentially selling clothing, they never neglected the medium: the dolls were exquisite.

So fashion and dolls have always gone hand in hand: little girls have always dressed, undressed, and dressed them again, often with garments their mothers and grandmothers lovingly sewed for them. Many small dolls are clad in hand-crocheted dresses and caps. Knitted wear made at home was not uncommon, and sometimes on an old doll, one may find dresses with uneven stitches and bits of crooked trim—such a thrill.

But on today's doll, it is the face which rivets the attention. The new dolls are so lifelike, a sensible person sometimes has to wonder: Is that woman holding a baby or a doll? In part, this is due to the great skill of the contemporary doll artists who have been given more freedom to exercise their creativity, and to the variety of materials now available.

Artists such as Robert Tonner, whose bridal Gillian is so exquisite, or Faith Wick's 1980s' Alice in Wonderland, are the products of years of formal art and fashion-design training.

Many also have backgrounds in costuming or graphics. Most of the new dolls exhibit the fine arts qualities of the new doll makers.

For a visual treat, if you like smaller dolls, feast your eyes on "Melissa" by Phyllis Seidl. The face of this doll is so delicate, so ethereal, she is glorious. There are others among contemporary doll makers and artists who deserve recognition, but in collecting, it all devolves into a matter of personal taste, and we can take comfort in the fact that most good doll artisans today are people of impeccable taste and achieving justifiable fame in their profession—their dolls are already considered heirlooms.

Most of the new artist-designers are venturing into these new channels to entice us with their skills by giving their dolls expressive faces, wonderful costumes, and different sizes, so we have a burgeoning world of beautiful and varied new dolls to choose from.

Indeed, our biggest problem is making choices; probably never before has such a wealth of talent presented so much beauty in doll form for us to collect. Prices for the most part are also reasonable, given the time and workmanship, as well as the many talents required to produce a desirable doll.

Some of these artist-designed dolls

A new musical version of Dolly Dingle designed by Bette Ball. Her name is L'il Dolly and she was made in a limited edition of 6,000. She has reddish-blonde hair and wears a red nightdress, with lace trim around a rounded yoke and along the bottom; green ribbon bows and pearls decorate the cuffs and center of the dress. She also has a matching nightcap, with lace edge and green bow. This doll wears a delightful pair of green-felt slippers, with holly on the toe. She carries a brass candle holder and a red velvet Christmas stocking with her name on it and a wooden bear inside. As if all that charm is not enough, she plays "I Saw Mommy Kissing Santa Claus." Value, $200-$250.

One of the cutest of the Dolly Dingle and Friends Dress-Up Party series, this is Melvis Bumps, an edition limited to 1,000. He is 10-1/2", all porcelain, with black hair. He is non-musical, articulated, and has light-blue double-acrylic eyes. He is wearing white boots, white knit stockings, and a sequined teal-color satin suit, with a wide white satin belt. His white shirt is also made of satin and the lapels are lined with white satin fabric; $250-$300.

This Dolly Dingle Jubilee Doll commemorates the 75th anniversary of Dolly's first appearance as a paper doll in 1913. She wears a simulated diamond-chip pendant to celebrate and the occasion is also noted on her neck stamp and hang tag. Her music box plays "Diamonds Are a Girl's Best Friend." She is, as the company says, "A collector's prize." At issue cost, $175. Value, $250-$350.

have appreciated in value well over many stock-market investments. Kay McKee, for example, who designs for one of the bigger houses, has seen her original selling prices spiral from hundreds of dollars to figures in the low thousands on secondary markets, and still moving upward.

This appreciation is a tribute not only to talent, but taste and an understanding of the field.

Among the new offerings–and there are almost too many to list–in the doll world, whimsy continues to surface. If you are planning a wedding, consider the individually sculpted figures of the actual bride and groom.

Made of porcelain, and expensive, you may have the bride depicted in all her actual wedding finery complete to the smallest detail of jewelry and hairstyle, antique lace, and even her bouquet. The groom looks as grooms usually do (don't ask the guests what the groom was wearing) in formal attire.

Another clever doll maker, Myla Fahn of Beverly Hills, Calif., works from photographs to craft what surely will become a treasured family remembrance. It is actually a wonderful use of the doll figure to document such a memorable occasion. When we consider that the Victorian wax, the bisque, even Celluloid top-of-the-wedding-cake dolls have survived and are now widely collected, think of these 50 years from now–a collection of figures representing real-life brides and grooms.

Any serious doll collector would certainly have to consider the artist-designer dolls currently being offered if value and investment is the goal. If living with beauty and delight is an equal goal, the variety of offerings by the current doll designers is an opportunity not to be missed.

Dolly Dingle dolls

Bette Ball and Karen Kennedy of Goebel North America are wonderful examples of today's talented and creative doll artists with solid backgrounds in fine arts and costume design.

The life-like dolls of Goebel and Victoria Ashlea are things of beauty on a different, more human artistic level. The attraction is not only their obvious beauty and quality, but their personal appeal. The artists strive to imbue each doll with life-like features, which strike a responsive chord in collectors.

This great skill in interpreting a child's innocence and sense of anticipation comes from a sincere love of, and for, children. Most successful doll artists confess to a liking, as well as love, of little ones and this translates to some of our most beautiful contemporary dolls.

The dolls produced by Goebel are among the best contemporary works and should already be considered heirlooms when purchased. This is a company totally conscious of the collector, so its products reflect accurately what doll collectors want.

Ball and her new Dolly Dingle dolls are a singular success. Nobody could ever resist Ms. Dingle, so Ball's new version brings to life an entrancing imp to captivate new generations. Dolly Dingle is a touch of sheer nostalgia, and collectors of any doll in this line are, above all, as my teen-age student puts it, "into nostalgia."

Their appeal really has to be seen to be believed. These dolls justifiably brought Ball a 1985 Doll of the Year Award.

Ball has a unique concept–she starts with fabric. She says that from a distance, the first notice of a doll is her clothing. "You have to get close to see the face, the wig, the other details," she says.

Since she is director of doll design for

Dolls made by Goebel of North America come complete with hand-numbered certificates of authenticity, hand-numbered description tags, a doll stand, tip sheet, and gift box. Each is back-stamped on back of the doll's neck. All the Dolly Dingles are limited-edition porcelain dolls, with fabric bodies, and all are dressed in the fashions and materials representing their original time period. They have hands, feet, and heads made of fine bisque porcelain. This is an original Dolly Dingle doll page by Grace Drayton.

Goebel USA, she has complete freedom to fashion any doll from the original sculpting to the final pat on the newly installed wig.

She feels dressing a doll requires a sense of what clothing could be worn by any human. Her dolls have been a spectacular success, so her philosophy of design is obviously accurate.

Kennedy has been designing under Ball's aegis since 1987. Her background in fashion blends admirably with Ball's approach. Kennedy, too, has won awards for her dolls and has had enormous success in this field.

Robert Tonner dolls

Today's craftspeople are not only well trained, but acutely aware of the particular demands of the doll market as it currently exists. So it is not difficult to understand that with their grasp of doll making itself, combined with this feel for the public pulse, they are attuned to provide exactly what doll collectors want. What collectors want, obviously, is a "pretty" or "interesting" doll with appropriate, attractive clothing.

If anyone on the planet fills those requirements, it has to be Robert Tonner. Tonner, whose dolls are so successful, says they reflect his experience in the fashion industry.

"I see dolls as mannequins. When I go to sculpt a new form, it is to expedite the clothing," he says. This is somewhat on the order of the French fashion doll, but with a difference.

Tonner has been quoted as saying he wants his dolls to be handled and "touchable." Some of his dolls have many changes of clothing, which can easily be put on or taken off. Tonner combines most of the great attractions of any desirable doll in his products: astonishing beauty of face and form,

wonderful costuming, and the most sought-after sizes; and while his dolls should, and will, be admired as treasures, they can also be considered durable if handled sensibly.

"Breathtaking" is the word for many of Tonner's dolls. They are so exciting, so magnificently dressed, they do literally take your breath away. His "fashion models" have such life-like faces as to be startling—they are very beautiful in the perfect high-fashion way. Tonner has an uncanny feel for his target area and an affinity for the exact nuances high-fashion models need to project.

Part of this is his background. From the Parsons School of Design in New York, he moved to Bill Blass as head designer. But his talents are not restricted to the fashion scene; his dolls include the classic characters of Little Orphan Annie, the revived Betsy McCall, and even Superman and Lois Lane.

He is a doll collector himself, which must, of course, influence any designer, but Tonner is a genuine star among the newer designers—his work really sparkles.

Celebrities are among his admirers: Actor Bruce Willis bid $50,000 for a doll dressed like Demi Moore. Tonner has won many awards and it is a rare opportunity for today's collectors to acquire, at a very reasonable price, a doll which is already a prize and whose future potential can only be imagined.

Tonner's dolls are all things to all serious collectors—just choose your category.

Seymour Mann dolls

The Connoisseur Collection by Seymour Mann is another example of a fine quality, award-winning doll collection sensibly priced and accessible through different kinds of stores, as well as the usual outlets.

This accessibility of such lovely new dolls, which reflect excellent, even outstandingly elegant costuming, as well as appealing doll faces and well-constructed bodies, is a great boon for collectors. It is, in fact, how I acquired my first Mann doll. I did not expect to encounter such a lovely doll in the particular store I bought it from.

In a full-page ad, which ran in 1994, Mann pictured seven adorable dolls, each a pronounced individual, aside from costume. Each has that special look—each face has different characteristics, as well as features.

To craft your doll collection so each example seems to have that unique face which all of us humans boast is a definite

This charming Dolly Dingle collection here and on the following page, by award-winning artist Bette Ball details with accuracy the charm of the original Dolly. As the company puts it, "These dolls, from their authentically designed costumes and exquisite detailing, to their soft bodies containing music boxes, every Dolly Dingle doll is a delightful representation of a mischievous charmer from the 1920s." The dolls are all numbered limited editions that originally sold for $60 to $140.

Left. Dolly Dingle 14" articulate. Plays "Catch a Falling Star," limited edition of 1,000. Value, $250-300.

Right. Toodles Dingle, 14", articulate. Plays "Teddy Bear's Picnic," and is a limited edition of 1,000. Value, $200-$250.

skill. Would every little girl want to look like Mann's Guinevere? Probably–she is a beautiful doll. But the Mann dolls present a variety of faces and leaves us choices–a real advantage to the collector.

These award-winning dolls are stunning and also affordable, which is certainly a plus in today's market. They have striking faces, gorgeous costumes, and can be collected in various sizes.

Many of the wonderful porcelain examples are already heirlooms.

The Mann dolls represent the spectrum–large, small, lavish costumes, some not quite so lavish but appealing anyway–and justifiably many of the dolls designed by Pamela Phillips have won prestigious awards.

This company, in spite of all the accolades its dolls have brought, is apparently determined to make its dolls accessible and so they can be found in stores other than doll shops and at doll shows. They have achieved much success and reached many new collectors this way. One only needs to take a careful look at 1994's "Allison" or "Su Lin" to realize how exquisite the Mann dolls can be.

Left. Kitty Cutie, a 13-1/2" limited edition of 1,000, plays "Pussy Cat, Pussy Cat." Value, $250-$295.

Right. Baby Bumps, a 12" limited edition of 1,000, plays "Thank Heaven for Little Girls." Articulate. Value, $275-$300.

These two "young citizens" of the Dingle Dell are Dolly's red-haired, green-eyed cousin Toodles Dingle, and her baby sister, Dotty Dumpling. They have the usual hang tags and a special-dated keepsake tag. Dotty is 12" and plays "Hush My Baby." Value, $200-$250. Toodles is 14", articulate, and plays "Make Someone Happy." Value, $200-$250.

Lolita, 42" tall, is a limited edition of 35 designed by Jan McLean of New Zealand. She is made of porcelain and would have to be the centerpiece of any collection. She is stunning and so limited in production as to be rare. McLean's dolls range in price from $2,000 to $12,000.

"Sweet Sweetie," a Dolly Dingle doll by Bette Ball, is a limited edition of only 1,000. She is 17", with the hat. She has light-green double-acrylic eyes, reddish-blonde hair, and her music is an appropriate "Put On a Happy Face." She wears a clown jumpsuit with a Halloween print and trimmed with a wide ruffle. The collar on her jumper is a ruff trimmed in green cording, and her cuffs and pant hems are trimmed in jingle bells and ribbon bows. Her matching pointed clown hat is trimmed with a pompom and ribbon streamers. She carries a mask on a stick and a treat bag. A wonderful holiday doll; $250-$300.

The Pleasant Company's 1997 holiday catalog announced a new member of its American Girls Collection: Josefina Montoya©, an Hispanic girl growing up in New Mexico in 1824. She has long mahogany brown hair, brown eyes that open and close, and a soft body, which is completely poseable. Measuring 18", she wears golden earrings and a traditional outfit of that area and time. All doll clothes have Velcro© closures. The 1998 catalog price for this doll and the hard-cover book is $82.

Vasilisha, by Brigette DeVal, is from the Georgetown Collection of Fairy Tales of Old Russia. The red-velvet folk costume on this doll is elegantly simple, her expression seems to see things we cannot fathom, and over all she embodies all the wonderful exotic attributes we look for in any doll, especially an international one. Vasilisha holds her own doll. This is part of a limited Artist's Edition. Value, $400-$450.

The versatility of modern doll designer Robert Tonner is evident in the beauty of this "ethnic" doll. Kwanza has the usual wonderful clothing of any Tonner doll, along with sandals, beads, and hoop earrings. She has startling deep brown glass eyes and black curly wig. This doll is number 42 of a limited edition of 500. Her costume is made of natural fibers and the hang tag advises that if it is "absolutely necessary, she can be wiped clean with a damp cloth." The collector is also advised to keep her out of direct sunlight, which should apply to almost all dolls. Kwanza is approximately 16" tall; $295-$450.

The magnificent face of Guinevere, made by Effanbee in 1995, dominates even the striking costume. Effanbee continues to produce desirable dolls and this one is outstanding. Made of porcelain. Value, $400-$500.

Ann Marie, who wears a colorful outfit, is by Jan Hagara; 14", 1992. B & J Co. Value, $450-$600.

you look too long at this hand-
ome Sinbad, those incredible eyes
ill mesmerize you. The doll is nicely
ressed and posed in keeping with
e theme. Neurnburger, 1996. This
oll is No. 20 of a limited edition of
.000 and comes with a certificate
authenticity; $200-$300.

Effanbee's Morning Glory Fairy is from the Storybook Series. She is made of vinyl and has poseable arms, legs, and head, and go-to-sleep eyes. This fairy also has painted toe nails. Value $50-$75.

The Royal Baby
THE PRIVATE LIFE OF
HIS ROYAL HIGHNESS
P·R·I·N·C·E W·I·L·L·I·A·M

I ♥ BUCKINGHAM PALACE

A PAPER DOLL BOOK♥
By Clarissa Harlowe and Cathy Camhy
Design: Sara Giovanitti · Illustration: Emanuel Schongut
PUBLISHED BY POCKET BOOKS NEW YORK · 49892·4·$4.95

Anyone interested in collecting memorabilia of royalty and was astute enough to invest in things to do with the children of the English royal family has made a very wise choice. This paper doll of Prince William is not particularly scarce yet, but it has great potential. It is a Pocket Books NY publication, designed by Clarissa Harlowe and Emanuel Schongut. Value, $18-$25.

This is a Gene doll from Ashton-Drake, by Mel Odom. This doll is quite popular: clubs have been formed in her name, there is a newsletter published about her, and there are conventions devoted to her. No wonder – she really is stunning and in that fey artistic way, Mr. Odom has caught the whole essence of the 1930s-'40s' movie star in one figure. Rather uncanny. Value, $150-$195 and rising.

These two bed dolls are part of a collection begun fairly recently. They are wearing their original clothes. Prices are uneven, but the starting price of any bed doll in good condition and with original clothes should be around $295, although prices are probably rising.

Miss Yokohama is Colorado's Japanese Friendship Doll. The Denver Museum of Miniatures, Dolls and Toys houses this beauty, but 16 of her sister dolls are still missing and all are considered priceless.

This elaborate and beautifully detailed figure is Chinese. Probably mythological, his luxurious silk robe, and the arrows, sword, staff, and crown, all indicate his high estate. This artistic, classical figure has a highly individualized face, which is memorable. Value, $400-$600.

Lara, by Kingstate Corp., is made of bisque porcelain and hand painted. A beautiful doll, she is dressed for ice skating and carries her skates. She is from the Prestige Collection. Instructions for the elaborate costume include dry clean only. Her hair can also be brushed (carefully). Value, $300-350.

These darling soft dolls are from the Heartfelt Collection. The details of the costuming are intriguing. Value, $125-$195.

There is no doubt that the Couture Collection by Madame Alexander is one of the company's gems. Look at Coco with the her dog Cleo. This doll comes with her own travel bag and wardrobe additions. Cleo is a masterful touch. Value, $400-$550, with accessories.

This bride and groom could only be bought at the annual Doll and Bear Show in Pasadena, California in 1997, the owner recalls. This would make for a very limited edition. Value, $100-$150, the pair.

This Patsy is like all the rest of the Effanbee remakes and a darling doll. Her costume looks vintage, but does not really justify the "flapper" tag; $95-$145.

This French fashion mannequin was designed by Mendel for the Théâtre de la Mode exhibition which toured the United States in 1946. The doll wears a full-length ermine cape lined in pale pink satin (synthetic). She also has a matching pink satin evening dress, with a strapless bodice and full skirt embroidered in a scroll pattern of old gold sequins. Coiffure: Desfossés. Embroidery: Gaby. Pale pink kid gloves: Hermés. Décor: Christian Bérard. (Photo courtesy Maryhill Museum of Art).

Tiffany, by Sandy Dolls, is from a limited edition of 750 in the Angels Series. A gorgeous doll, she is delicate and beautiful and has a heavenly look, even to the graceful pose of the hands; $600-$800.

A Show Stoppers' show stopper, Zena is elaborately costumed in vivid shades of purple and gold. From the Enchanted Art Collection Series. Value, $175-$200.

Hans, by T.J. Collections, is approximately 9". Made in Thailand, the doll has ceramic face and hands and cloth body. His face is rather expression-less, but his costume is very well done. Value, $35-$55.

This Woman Marine is from the Alexander Armed Forces Collection. Value, $85-$125.

Although they are not dolls themselves, bears are a big part of doll collecting. Jack Frost, shown here, was made in a limited edition of 75 brown bears. He is sitting on an impressive polar bear, but each figure can be sold separately. This is No. 16 of 75. Pair, $600-$650.

Doll accessories add so much to a doll collection and are therefore highly collectible. This child's China cabinet, c. 1890-1910, has two drawers, double-glass doors, and original hardware. It measures 23" high, 13" wide, and 7-1/4" deep. This is a difficult piece to find and values between $400-$450. The cabinet holds a miniature Wedgwood Beatrix Potter tea set, which values at $250.

This all-bisque Cabbage Patch Kid on a stand has a value between $150-$195. Cabbage Patch Kids are making a comeback, although the bisque ones do not seem to be as popular as the soft-body types.

Individual characters from the popular FOX TV show, "The Simpsons," such as Bart, can be found on the market in various sizes and for various prices, ranging from $25-$50 and perhaps quite higher.

Especially adorable are this bride and groom, Billie Bumps and Dolly Dingle. Billie is 14", articulate, and plays "I'm Sitting on Top of the World." Dolly herself is 13" and plays Mendelsohn's "Wedding March." Both are limited editions of 1,000. The 1990 value, $500-$600, the pair.

These Dolly Dingle friends are Cherry Blossom, 14", articulate, and plays "I'd Like to Teach the World to Sing"; and Lindy Bumps, who is 12", articulate, and plays "Tea for Two." Both dolls are limited editions of 1,000 and value between $200-$250.

Stunningly beautiful porcelain dolls have been created for Victoria Ashlea Originals© by Karen Kennedy and Bette Ball. This doll, Andrea, by Karen Kennedy, stands 10" tall, and is a limited edition of 2,000. Value, $275-$325.

These are part of the Tiny Tots and Tiny Clowns Collection for Victoria Ashlea by Karen Kennedy. All have been issued in editions of 2,000 worldwide and all are 10". From left are Stacy, Megan, Danielle, Lisa, Lindsey, and Marie. Retailed in 1993 for around $40, they now have a value of $195-$225. All have porcelain hand-painted faces and life-like eyes. Each doll is marked with a Victoria Ashley Original© backstamp and each has a certificate of authenticity and a hang tag. Tiny Tots and Tiny Tots Clown dolls are limited to no more than 2,500 worldwide and cost between $29.50-$200.

These Victoria Ashlea Originals© by Karen Kennedy are all 10" tall, limited to 2,000 worldwide and are named Christine, Shawna, Monique, Susan, and Patricia. Beautifully dressed with fine materials and enhanced with laces, faux jewels, and other attractive trims, they each have a value between $250-$300.

The dolls pictured here and on the previous page, are mint in the box, and once they appear on the secondary market, prices escalate because of their limited editions. The Seymour Mann Doll company provides a good opportunity for any collector to own a fine doll at reasonable prices.

Tiffany, who wears no hat, is smaller and dressed all in blue with lace. Notice the pink shoelaces. This attention to detail is a hallmark of these dolls. Value, $95-$150.

Caroline, from the Connoisseur Collection, is a very pretty doll cocooned in pink and lace wearing a large hat with lace trim; she even wears stockings. She comes with a hang tag with all pertinent information and is a limited edition of 2,500. Actual retail price, $150-$195.

Another member of the Connoisseur Doll Collection, Patsy wears old rose and lace, has particularly striking eyes, and a gorgeous head of hair. Limited edition of 2,500. Value, $250-$300.

Madame Pompador is also a member of the Connoisseur Doll Collection by Seymour Mann and among a limited edition of 7,500. Value, $300-$325.

Robert Tonner dolls present a modern-day look at the fashion doll. His skills are so finely honed, his dolls represent the best of doll sculpture, as well as more than could ever be expected in the fashion realm. His dolls run the gamut of characters, all exhibiting truly fine workmanship and a clever diversity of interpretation as he moves from one area to another. If you admire excellence, look at Robert Tonner dolls.

Karin is 19" and made of porcelain. She is wearing a seagreen shantung gown, embroidered with gold flowers and tiny gold sequins and beads. Her auburn hair is beautifully styled in an updo, dotted with gold fabric roses. Tonner's porcelain dolls retail from the low to the high hundreds of dollars.

Daphne is 19" and made of vinyl. She wears a ball gown of cream and gold brocade, topped by a layer of jeweled net. Her cropped bolero is encrusted with sequins and pearls. Her hair is elaborately styled in a top knot of curls and she wears a pearl and crystal necklace and bracelet. Current 1998 retail price is $345.

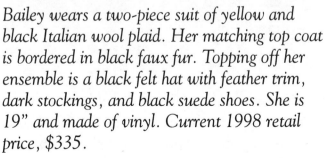

Bailey wears a two-piece suit of yellow and black Italian wool plaid. Her matching top coat is bordered in black faux fur. Topping off her ensemble is a black felt hat with feather trim, dark stockings, and black suede shoes. She is 19" and made of vinyl. Current 1998 retail price, $335.

Las Vegas Show Girl, 19" and vinyl. She is wearing a fuschia velvet, pink satin and metallic gold lace costume with a floor-length train lined in pink satin. Her blonde hair is styled in an updo, crowned with a spectacular headdress of gold jewels and a pink ostrich plume. She wears gold fishnet stockings and strappy gold heels. In 1997, a prestigious toy retailer asked Tonner to attend the opening of its flagship store in Las Vegas. He designed this limited-edition doll, "Vegas showgirl model," for this event.

Another aspect of Tonner's talent is the Betsy McCall doll he sculpted for a new version of the beloved doll of the 1950s. She is high-quality vinyl and crafted especially for collectors. There are all sorts of accessories to complement Betsy: clothing, a trunk, a pet dog, even a bed to give her a place to wear her lovely "bed duo" set.

This is Betsy McCall.

This Is Betsy's Cousin Barbara.

This Is Betsy's Cousin Linda.

Betsy McCall, left, is 14", vinyl, and has brown hair. She can also be found with red hair in the same size vinyl doll. Here she wears pink check with white strap sandals and hair ribbon. The dolls are available for a selling price of $79.95, but already secondary-market prices have shown an increase to $110-$125. The center doll is Betsy's cousin Barbara, who wears blue check, white sandals, and hair ribbons on her blonde hair. She is vinyl and 10" tall. This doll is still available for a selling price of $79.95, but the secondary-market value is $110-$125. Betsy's cousin Linda, in a lilac-check dress, is 14" and vinyl. This doll is still available at a retail price of $77.95, but the secondary-market value is $110-$125.

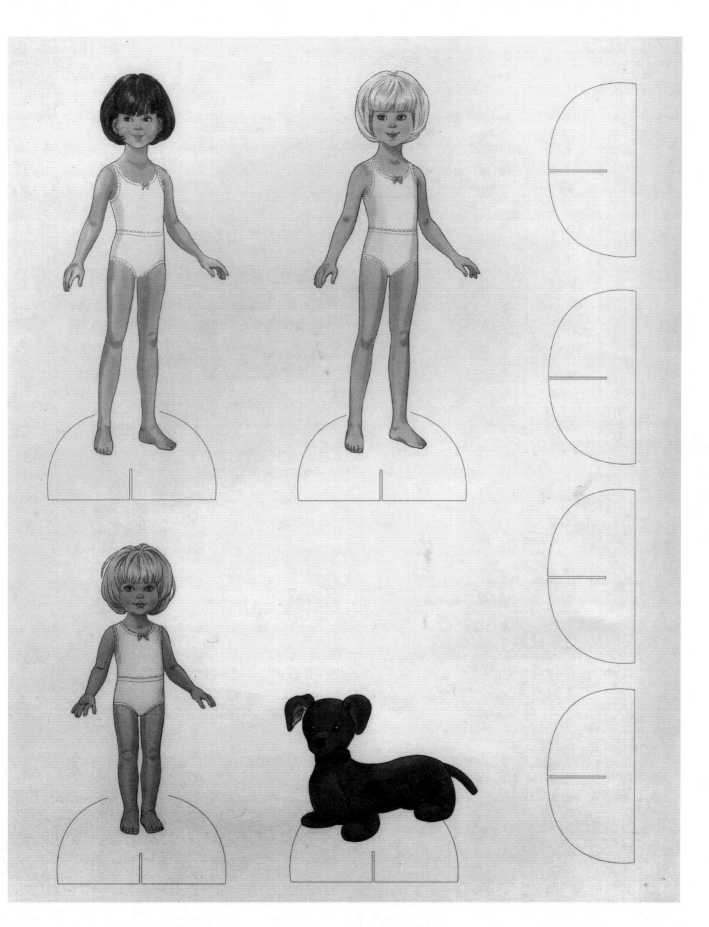

Tonner's paper dolls of this new Betsy, shown on this page and the next three, are captivating with beautiful art work. These are worthy of the best paper-doll collection.

"Making Gingerbread"
Betsy goes to grandma's house to help with the holiday gingerbread.

Style #98530

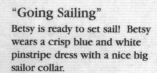

"Going Sailing"
Betsy is ready to set sail! Betsy wears a crisp blue and white pinstripe dress with a nice big sailor collar.

Style #98531

Betsy's "It's Cold Outside" Outfit
Betsy loves to sit by the fire in her cozy hand knit sweater and matching cap. Even while keeping warm she can be stylish in socks, boots, and tights that compliment her outfit.

Style #98537

"Rainy Days"
Betsy is ready for any rainy day in her print raincoat with matching umbrella.

Style #98532

"Pretty in Pink"

Betsy looks so glamorous for her first formal dance! She wears a pink tulle and velvet gown.

Style #98533

Betsy's "Earth Day" Outfit

Betsy loves to spend time outside and she is very aware of the environment. She wears a printed cotton windbreaker over her "save the planet" t-shirt. Jeans and red sneakers complete her outfit that includes her pretend fishing pole and fish!

Style #98534

"Getting Dressed"

Betsy has everything she needs to be party pretty. Betsy's Getting Dressed outfit includes an undershirt, panties, and a lace trimmed full slip. Also included are tights, white shoes and a brush and mirror set.

Style #98536

"Betsy Learns to Sew"

Betsy can't wait to start her first sewing project. She wears a cotton smock with "thread" print and a tape measure bow! Shoes, socks, glasses, and scissors complete her outfit.

Style #98535

As usual with Robert Tonner, the costumes for even his paper dolls are exceptional, as this page and the next one illustrate.

"Holiday Twosome"

Betsy and Linda dress up for the holiday in their red velvet dresses. Bright taffeta bows give these dresses a festive holiday look! Also included are white tights and red velvet shoes.

Style #98538

"Walking Nosey"

Betsy loves to take Nosey for a walk no matter what the weather is outside. She is wearing her corduroy parka with black tights and snow boots. Nosey has a matching outfit also!

Style #98540

"Bedtime Duo"

Betsy and her cousin Linda love sleep - overs! They snuggle into bed, with Betsy in her teddy bear printed nightgown and Linda in her two piece pajamas.

Style #98539

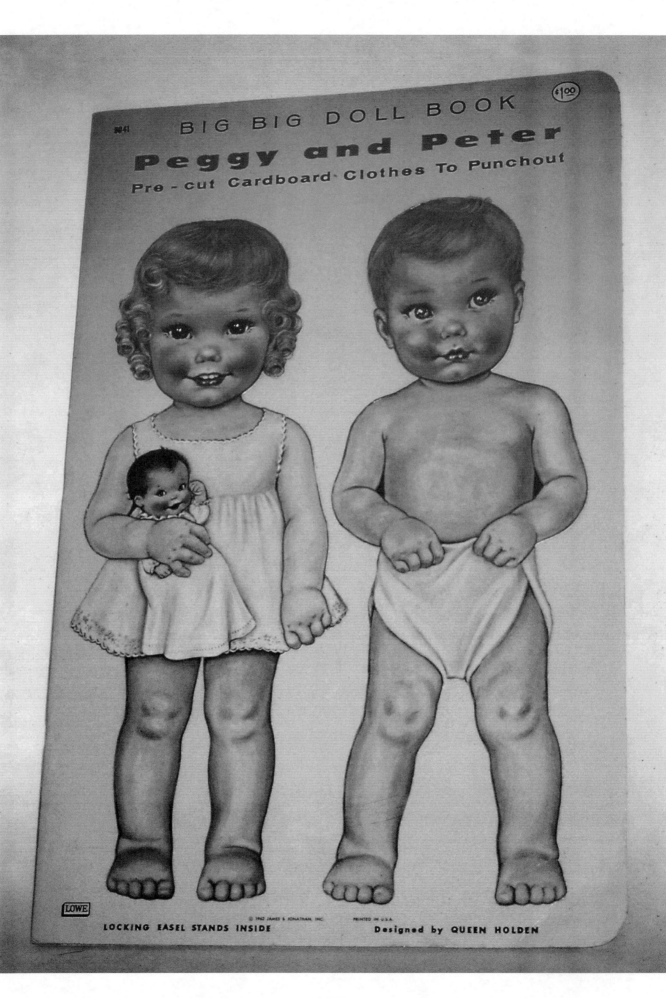

Paper Dolls

One of the greatest attributes of paper dolls has always been price. Even in the depths of the Depression, an occasional book of paper dolls was affordable. Another great plus is ease of storage; still another is portability.

Of course, the main attraction is the representation itself, plus the emphasis on costume and the fun of setting up the dolls and changing that costume.

Marketing specialists will tell you that interaction between the buyer and the products they buy produces a happy customer. So paper dolls, probably unwittingly, have this wonderful attribute of totally involving the child with the toy.

The new collectibility of paper dolls has not much altered the affordability of new paper dolls. Anyone who collects Disney can hardly keep up with its production of current stars of its movies, animal or human, in paper versions. The Tierney paper dolls also will not stress the budget. It is still fun, although many adult collectors no longer consider them playthings and refuse to cut them as the maker intended. Paper dolls which have been cut usually have minimal value, unless the depiction is so rare it commands extra attention for whatever reason.

In the current market, celebrity paper dolls are probably the most popular. They are doing well at auction, selling well on the Internet and in shops, and collectors will pay top dollar for certain personalities.

In the days of yore, little girls were not always so particular. At times I have bought notebooks or old catalogs, with figures cut from magazines, newspapers or even precious old books, which some child has pasted in the book (rather haphazardly) directly over the original text, then cut clothing advertisements from various sources and pasted them in alongside. This is childish ingenuity at its highest level—no sophisticated paper-doll books were available, so children had to make their own.

Paper dolls were a source of great amusement to children, but since television, home videos, and movies have become so accessible, contemporary paper dolls as a major plaything have almost phased out of the doll picture.

It's a tribute to adult collectors that

The eternal Raggedy Ann and Andy in paper, right. These characters can be found as paper dolls in many guises, so if you like these dolls, you have a whole spectrum from which to collect their paper-doll images. Uncut condition by Whitman, 1962, original selling price 49 cents. Bought in 1994 for $10, but prices are entirely variable. The value today is $28-$35, as everything to do with these wonderful dolls with their marvelous storied backgrounds continues to attract new collectors. The Rock-Star dolls are appreciating rapidly. The period has more or less ended and if you missed the paper dolls as they whizzed by, you'll have to look a bit to find them today since they are not so abundant. This set is by Golden and the graphics are impressive. Uncut. Bought in 1996 for $8. Recent prices of similar, but not exact duplicates, have been $15-$20.

the hobby has regenerated. Characters from books we loved, those of newspaper fame when we were children, or classic films are part of the past which all of us are trying to recapture.

Those who had the great good fortune to be teen-agers in the 1940s remember those irreplaceable actors and actresses who kept us so enthralled–June Allyson, Judy Garland, Vivian Leigh as Scarlett O'Hara, and that ultimate pin-up Betty Grable. Their paper images are remarkably well done; the faces and figures quite accurate. Some years ago, the Gone With the Wind paper-doll book made by Merrill in 1940 and in uncut condition, was valued at about $400.

Most of the famous people of bygone eras have had paper dolls fashioned in their likeness and there are many very large collections of these "celebrity dolls" in paper.

These inexpensive paper keepsakes represent a unique segment of American history–although paper dolls were popular in Europe before Americans took them seri-ously–and have certainly proved a good investment.

More such collections are turning up at auctions, although somehow it must be wrenching to part with one's paper dolls. There is something about having the paper item itself; it is a feeling not lightly transmitted by mere words; it is subtle and highly emotional. Often it is a person who loves books, as well as dolls, who is a collector of such paper ephemera.

If your sensibility does not run to emotional involvement with a relatively minor collectible (pricewise at least) such as paper dolls, you probably will find this not easily understood; but there is indeed something about collecting paper dolls which goes beyond the doll and the costume.

It is basically the same reaction you have to a doll you love, but it has a slightly different focus; and as doll collecting becomes more expensive, paper dolls become more desirable.

It is easy to dismiss the collecting of paper dolls as a fairly insignificant aspect of

The Nixon era is a burgeoning collectible time frame on its own, so these paper dolls have value in many directions—as paper dolls, political memorabilia, and part of a First Ladies-First Family collection—as part of a doll collection. These are very well done, the images are amazingly accurate, and this type is also getting expensive. Top: White House Paper dolls by Saalfield, 1970, as is the book at lower left, devoted exclusively to Tricia Nixon. These two examples are indicative of how interesting a paper-doll collection can be: the portrayals are lovely, the backgrounds imaginative, the subject matter important. These are somewhat scarce and the value of each, uncut, is $30-$35. Right: An older book picturing two stand-up models and called Dollies Fashion Show. Costing 29 cents at issue, uncut now are $20-$25. Bottom right: The ever-popular celebrity doll, even in paper. The beautiful depictions of Rex Harrison and Audrey Hepburn, while not precisely lifelike as are the Nixon women, are stunning nonetheless. "My Fair Lady" is such an everlasting musical, probably new dolls will be issued from time to time. These are uncut and valued at $22-$30.

doll collecting, but paper dolls have been made and played with for centuries. Commercially, paper dolls succeeded in the 19th century when more money and more leisure time was becoming available to the rising middle class. These two factors led to each town beginning to boast an "emporium." Often, these precious books of dolls were given away as advertising. Imagine that.

Supposedly, the first commercially successful paper doll was made in the image of Jenny Lind, the Swedish Nightingale in the 1850s. She was a true sensation in her time and inspired every kind of collectible you can think of—and so paper dolls must have seemed a fitting tribute to her enormous popularity.

The concept then was to provide an image of the singer, so little girls could appreciate her talent, beauty, and her costumes, even though they never expected to see her or hear her sing. No one thought of saving these dolls for their value—no one could possibly have foreseen the hefty price rises of the 1990s. Now the concept is to aim your paper doll at the collector; very few of them are bought for little girls anymore and most of them are put away uncut.

It is well to remember that the publishers of some of these dolls have become household words: McLoughlin Bros., Raphael Tuck of London, and the Dennison Co., among others. McLoughlin Bros. published the well-known Tom Thumb and his wife, she with her trousseau. Then, as now, they used well-known people for their dolls so they might be considered the original celebrity paper-doll makers.

You can collect in any segment of this field: bridal paper dolls, royal paper dolls, Betsy McCall or any other of the popular magazine dolls, of course any era

Saalfield made these interactive paper dolls. The costumes "lace on" and were made for girls 4 to 9. The dolls are on heavy board and the costumes came in sheets. There is really something special about paper dolls; look carefully at the faces and clothing of the little girls. There is also variety beyond just a flat figure. These came boxed and are still in their original box and in excellent condition; $45-$55.

celebrity dolls, fairy-tale paper dolls. The choices seem endless, and all collectors probably realize that this is a market in which you have to keep current. Watch all book stores, as well as discount stores, for contemporary figures–these dolls have a very short shelf life.

Did you notice the Twiggy doll, for instance, during her short stay in the stores in the late 1960s and early 1970s? If you don't remember Twiggy, the famous fashion model, you have discovered the attraction and value of paper-doll collecting: Who and when are important, and buying it when you see it is essential.

Prices are uneven in this field, so much depends on condition. Age is not necessarily the best determinant, since celebrity dolls of the '30s and '40s are enjoying great popularity at the moment; but a really old paper doll in good condition is never to be ignored. Even though these older paper dolls are being temporarily bypassed by more collectors because they are higher priced, they can be a good investment–often selling for hundreds of dollars to the serious collector.

Take the dolls of the Palmer Cox Brownie figures, for example. Cox patented 12 Brownie figures in 1882; today, his uncut books of these same figures will sell for many hundreds of dollars each and are

going up all the time. There are unsubstantiated reports that one book sold a few years ago for more than $1,000.

It is always important to look carefully through paper memorabilia when attending estate sales and auction previews–sometimes real treasures tend to get buried among the more mundane–but for this you need time and knowledge.

Paper dolls are becoming an integral part of collecting the real doll itself, since many collectors are beginning to surround their dolls with compatible artifacts and often the doll will be flanked by its paper counterpart (uncut, of course). This makes for interesting display.

Display can be troublesome. One excellent way to keep your dolls clean and flat is with a separate dresser or cabinet with large drawers. It is no problem to open these drawers to exhibit your collection; but, of course, the size of the collection might make this impractical unless they are kept as separate categories, each type to its own drawer.

You can separate your books by personality, time or fashions in these drawers, and it is then an easy matter to open the correct drawer to any specific subject or personality if your friends have preferences, and you really have no worries if the room is not excessively damp.

A variation but still considered within the paper-doll category, these are wood dolls with "Round About Dresses" which came with their own scissors. Again, the graphics are marvelous, with beautiful little girls and darling animals. These also came boxed. By Milton Bradley. In original box, excellent condition; $45-$50.

Paper dolls are beginning to inspire passion in collectors and when that happens, the marketplace begins to look very attractive; so never pass up an interesting paper doll in good condition—you will find yourself totally entranced, and who knows what the future holds?

While you are storing this new collectible of yours, enjoy it and be content to wait. It is not eating or drinking anything, it is totally cost free, and you may be surprised at the pleasure and profit it may bring.

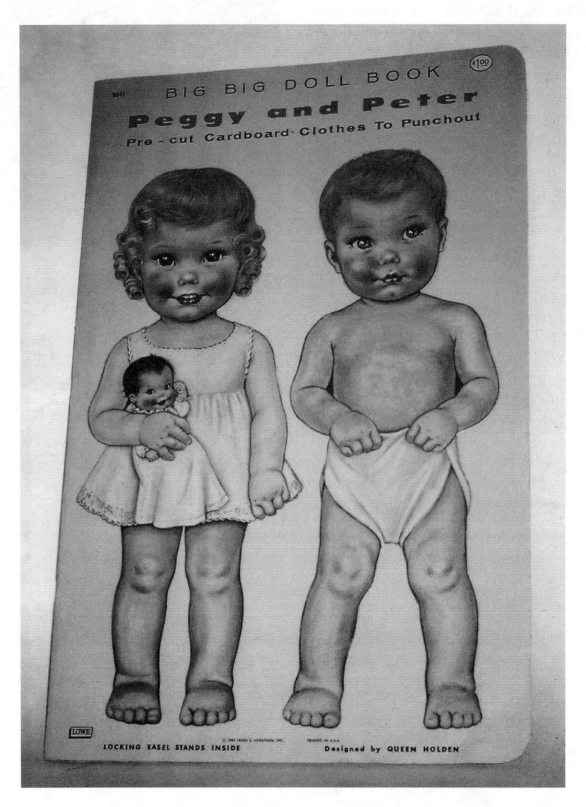

One of the giant paper-doll books, Peggy and Peter. Sold originally for $1, which was rather high at the time, these had pre-cut "punch-out clothes." Peggy is carrying a most adorable doll. These were designed by Queen Holden and made by Lowe; $45-$65. Many collectors consider these very large paper dolls to be a separate category, but no thinking collector would be deterred from any purchase by a detail such as that. Price and condition, yes; but other considerations when you see a desirable paper doll are irrelevant.

Two Little Girls on easel-base stands. Another large paper doll book by Lowe. Again one girl holds a doll; wonderful price of $45-$55.

Patterns

Doll collectors are now beginning to concern themselves with old patterns, once the province of the vintage-clothing collector; doll clothing repair people; the home hobby needle person; and the specialized collectors of Halloween costumes, Easter themes, or patterns featuring children's fashions.

Now the hunt is on in a very big way for old patterns, contemporary to the doll itself and featuring clothing for that particular doll. This area is still a fairly inexpensive way to ease into the doll field, although a few years ago prices started to rise and continue to escalate. Now a good pattern for specific dolls can rarely be bought for under $10, and depending on the doll it relates to, the cost can be much higher.

This is a particularly interesting tangent to doll collecting, even if you do not sew or own the original doll. It is fun, storage and display are easy, and if you search carefully while bargains still exist, you will soon have a worthwhile collection.

The hunt itself is challenging and will take you to thrift shops, house sales, and other places you might not go, as well as some shops which are now beginning to acknowledge the importance of these old patterns. Most bigger doll shows also now feature a selection of patterns.

One of the greatest gifts collecting dolls bestows on us is awareness of the ever-changing world we move in. The fairly sudden popularity of patterns points to the necessity to think in wide terms, to always be aware of anything new, and as a collector, even if you collect only the doll itself, always try to increase your knowledge and appreciation of that doll's particular world. That is what makes us interesting; that is what keeps us ageless.

Old doll patterns have slowly been building a collecting base. Of all the older clothing patterns issued by the well-known companies, the doll patterns are probably the most difficult to find and often have actually been used for their original purpose, so they can be shabby. They are now being bought by collectors of the dolls themselves; the Cabbage Patch Kids, for example. Collectors of large dolls have long been buying patterns of baby clothes in order to dress their own dolls, but now the

Here is an example of how these patterns tie into a doll collection even if you personally can't sew a button on. This example is not in perfect condition, but is adequate either for research or as a "go with" for your collection or if you are a serious seamstress. I paid $3 each for these in 1997. Both envelopes read, "Clothes for your Cabbage Patch Kids" and one includes a transfer for you to iron on. Value, $8-$12.

patterns are collectible on their own.

They are a wonderful adjunct to any collection for the information they impart. As with most of the older dolls, these patterns were considered a teaching tool. The Raggedy Ann is actually labeled a "Teach Me Wardrobe for Raggedy Ann and Andy." It reads, "Garments are designed to give practice in lacing and tying and in opening and closing zippers, buttons and snaps. The belt, trimmed with a tape measure, gives numbers practice." What a wonderful, innovative idea way back in 1971. This pattern still bears the current

selling price of $12.

It is still a good way to begin, or even to set out to acquire these to complement your doll collection. It is fun, storage and display is easy and if you search carefully while bargains still exist, you will soon have a worthwhile collection.

The old dress patterns have been slowly gathering a following for some time now. It is a bit like collecting postcards or books: it takes much time, so some collectors become frustrated. This is unfortunate because there are little treasures among the dross.

An excellent example of the kind of pattern to search for, this is a McCall's Printed Pattern, which is geared specifically for a diminutive doll's wardrobe like Ginny, Muffie, Lingerie Lou, or Dolly Dolly. This is pretty enough to be framed and placed near your collection if you own any of these dolls. Price, $15-$22.

What is most desirable for doll collectors are the older patterns for doll clothes and vintage baby clothes, which may fit their own dolls.

What has always been a No. 1 priority for pattern collectors, long before the new developments, was the dedicated hunting by vintage clothing people, clothing restorers, and really avid children's-costume collectors. The old patterns can be wonderful for all these, but now we doll collectors are on our own quest.

All the big companies made such patterns, so they are not scarce, but should be in good, if not necessarily perfect, condition and intact.

They are still underpriced. But not for long.

McCalls' Maggie Reggie stuffed doll and wardrobe, 1957. Cute doll and marvelous wardrobe. This says, "clothes also fit manufactured diminutive dolls 7 to 8 inches." It was easy, too; you just had to stamp the transfer on the fabric and cut out. Because the seller felt this was of some consequence to somebody back in 1989 when I bought it, it was in a plastic envelope with a Do Not Open Sign. The price, $3.50, seemed very high then when collecting old patterns was rather esoteric, but the value now is $15-$20.

Sunrubber

Sun Rubber produced some of the cutest dolls ever made and they are becoming wildly collectible. In June of 1977, Sue Ellen Folk of Sun Products Corporation wrote me that "Sun Rubber, now Sun Products Corporation, discontinued the manufacture of rubber dolls some twenty years ago" and that "since a move to Georgia...many records were thrown away before the move."

The bane of the collector of the earlier American toys is the dearth of definitive company records. Most of these toys were so inexpensive when originally sold, the companies felt that they were expendable and that keeping long-term records for such goods was unnecessary and cumbersome.

But there is no doubt about it: Sun Rubber was a company which had a relatively long life, survived the Great Depression, and gave generations of children pleasure. It made not only the dolls, but adorable animals, and cooperated with Disney to produce Mickey Mouse, Donald Duck in his rubber car, and even Dumbo.

The company made a very successful line of cars and trucks, now somewhat scarce. Sun Rubber began with little knowledge of the field it was about to conquer, but it soon discovered what children wanted. The company's products were successful, well made, and all are now collectible.

Thomas Smith, who founded the company in 1923, had no particular knowledge of dolls or toys and bought the Avalon Rubber Company of Barberton, Ohio as a speculative venture. The speculation was floundering. None of the products the company was making was terribly successful, so the employees were involved in attempts to come up with salable rubber items which would be inexpensive to manufacture and could be sold at a low price.

Records indicate it was actually an employee (as is so often the case, with success credited to the tycoons) who rescued the ailing company by suggesting that a doll-sized hot-water bottle might be tried. Sales were rather phenomenal for this little accessory and since Woolworth's liked the idea and ordered thousands, there was no doubt of its success.

Even today, one marvels at the detail and accuracy of the little bottle and now the dolls are rising in price as collectors realize they are truly things of the past, adorable, unbreakable, and small enough not to require a six-bedroom house to be displayed properly. Many accessories came with the dolls and these, too, are something to be coveted.

These adorable small rubber dolls have taken a long time to reach their potential.

They were enormously popular playthings, sold prodigiously well, many have been lost by attrition due to the properties of the rubber itself, but many did survive in excellent condition and we should consider ourselves lucky to be able to buy them today. They are an example of the ultimate play doll: entertaining to children and indestructible in the ordinary way. It is almost unbelievable that these darlings languished for so long and were almost ignored.

It is not often the word "cute" really applies—it is used to describe everything even when inappropriate—but the company itself designated these dolls as "cute" and the term is just as apt now as it was then.

Several large collections began simply because the prices were so low for so long. One collector confesses to never having paid more than $3 to $5 for any Sun Rubber doll until four years ago, when prices began to spiral upward. Her last acquisition—the doll and all the accessories—cost $100. She bought all these dolls originally because she remembered them, owned a few from childhood, the price was right, and most important, essentially for her own pleasure with no future profit in mind. She feels her motives were pure and she is being rewarded. Facetious, of course, but the elements of truth inherent in all intelligent collecting are there.

Sun Rubber's advertising emphasized the educational aspect of its toys. The Buttons & Bows Sewing Kit promotional material stated it was "the most educational sewing outfit ever offered." It is obvious that some doll manufacturers felt an obligation to make toys which taught, as well as entertained.

The one drawback to these darlings is their basic material. If the rubber toy is not kept in a room with a stable temperature, it will deteriorate. I have lost several dolls to excessive heat. They are also subject to punctures and tearing when weakened, so use some caution when storing.

Much earlier, Goodyear Rubber Co. actually manufactured dolls with rubber heads and cloth bodies, but these are rarely found and even more rarely found with the heads in good condition. The production numbers of these were small.

For ten years, Sun Rubber dolls were available everywhere for small sums of money, but are now costing a minimum of $35 each and rising, although here and there a bargain can still be found. These cuties deserve their success, and that unsung hero and his great idea of the hot-water bottle deserves our kudos.

a word about "Sunbabe" DOLLS

FEEDING

SUNBABES drink water easily and have no complicated assembly that might break or puncture.

CHANGING

SUNBABES' molded rubber bodies will not absorb water; will not deteriorate from long-wet diapers or bathing.

DRESSING

Completely movable joints allow arms, legs and the head to turn to any position for easy dressing.

SLEEPING

True-to-life plastic eyes, whether stationary or sleeping, are firmly, individually locked inside the head.

"Amosandra"
No. 10026

Beloved 10-inch colored doll of Amos 'n Andy fame . . . Drinks and wets . . . Cries when squeezed . . . Has own bottle and wears a bright bib and diaper . . . Head, arms and legs are turnable . . . Stationary brown plastic eyes . . . Color permanently cured in the rubber . . . Hair, mouth and cheek decoration sprayed on in washable paints . . . Individually boxed for display . . . Packed 1 dozen per carton . . . Weight: 13½ lbs.

*"Amosandra" is a trademark of the Columbia Broadcasting System, Inc. The doll is an "Amos 'n Andy" article, conceived by T. W. Smith, Jr., designed by Ruth E. Newton, and manufactured by The Sun Rubber Company under a design copyright of the Columbia Broadcasting System, Inc.

"So-Wee"
No. 10041

Smallest of SUN's flesh-colored jointed dolls, So-Wee is size-designed for the youngest of little mothers . . . 10 inches tall . . . A completely tubbable rubber doll . . . Stationary plastic eyes can't fall or be plucked out . . . Falls and bumps won't break her . . . Wets her diaper and drinks from own bottle . . . Has squeeze voice . . . Wears colorful bib and diapers . . . Attractively packaged . . . Shipped 1 doz. per carton . . . Weight: 13 lbs.

© Ruth E. Newton

"Cindy Lee"
No. 10039

Twelve inches of rubber doll cuteness . . . Dressed in flattering sunsuit and bonnet . . . Blows soap bubbles from her pipe . . . Drinks from her bottle and wets . . . Fully jointed . . . Locked-in stationary plastic eyes . . . Decorated with non-toxic paints . . . Will not deteriorate with bathing . . . Packaged for attention-getting display . . . Shipped 1 doz. to carton . . . Weight: 17 lbs.

Cindy Lee Blows Bubbles too!

Catalog pages like this and the ones on the following pages are a real plus to collectors since they are original company literature and not magazine pages. Sun Rubber dolls are still a good buy; some more than others, so at least take a look at them. Any 1953 Sunbabe doll should have a starting price of $35-$45; dressed dolls have a value of $50-$60; and dolls with their original cases should start at $125 and can go as high as $195. The company designated its dolls not only by name, but by number. It is a tremendous addition to research to have this kind of information. Amosandra, top, is today valued at $300-$350; So-Wee, middle, is valued at $45-$55; and Cindy Lee, bottom, has a value of $45-$55.

Tod-L-Twins

No. 14038

Double sales power in this set . . . Boy and girl standing vinyl dolls with squeeze voices and stationary plastic eyes . . . Both 10½ inches tall, washable and dressable . . . Wear matching play togs, with simulated underclothing and molded shoes and socks . . . Displayed in artistic window box with handle . . . Packed ½ doz. per carton . . Weight: 10½ lbs.

© The Sun Rubber Co.

© Ruth E. Newton

"So-Wee"

SET

No. 10541

Cuddlesome So-Wee, the 10-inch rubber doll with the drink-wet-cry features, comes surrounded by accessories to amuse and educate . . . There's a hot water bottle, nursing bottle, rattle, bib, teething ring, soap and soap dish . . . She wears a diaper . . . All show in the window box . . . Shipped ½ doz to carton . . . Weight: 11½ lbs.

"So-Wee" Blows Bubbles too!

"Betty Bows"

No. 10044

Sunbabe Betty Bows is a 12-inch, flesh-colored rubber doll . . . Turnablye vinyl head and movable arms and legs . . . Sleeping eyes are long-lashed . . . Drinks, wets, cries and sleeps . . . Entirely washable . . . Dressed in bright sunsuit with ribbon tied through hair . . . Nursing bottle included . . . Gift-box packaged . . . Shipped 1 doz. per carton . . . Weight: 15 lbs.

© The Sun Rubber Co.

"Babee-Bee"

No. 10024

A big favorite is real-as-life Babee-Bee . . . 13 inches long, she has a vinyl head with sleeping eyes and a rubber body with natural moving limbs . . . Drinks from her bottle, wets her diaper, cries when squeezed and sleeps at naptime . . . Wears a smart, fully-cut coat, bootees and diaper . . . Individually boxed . . . Shipped ½ doz. to carton . . . Weight: 9½ lbs.

© Ruth E. Newton

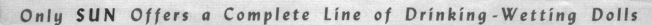

Only SUN Offers a Complete Line of Drinking-Wetting Dolls

New Drinking-Wetting

"Betty Bows"
No. 10046

The only rubber doll that wears a ribbon through her hair . . . Warm-toned, movable vinyl head on fully-jointed rubber body . . . 12 inches tall . . . Blows bubbles, drinks, wets, sleeps and cries . . . Life-like, locked-in plastic eyes are long-lashed . . . Dressed in saucy sun dress, bonnet and bootees . . . Bubble pipe and nursing bottle are included . . . Attractively packaged . . . Shipped ½ doz. per carton . . . Weight: 12 lbs.

No. 10046

© The Sun Rubber Co.

No. 10027
© Ruth E. Newton

Advertised in LIFE

"Babee-Bee"
No. 10027

Sweet-faced, lovable and absolutely tubbable, Babee-Bee is 13 inches long . . . Sleeping eyes are anchored in vinyl head . . . Unbreakable rubber body features SUN's exclusive, waterproof joints . . . Cries, blows bubbles, wets and drinks . . . A prize baby doll in her layette-style sacque, knitted panties and bootees . . . Bubble pipe, soap, nursing bottle and bib are accessories . . . Boxed for sales-promoting display . . . Shipped ½ doz. to carton . . . Weight: 13½ lbs.

Cindy Lee Formula Set

No. 10625

Perfect set for imitative play . . . Contained in a sturdy carrying case are: four rubber-nippled nursing bottles in a wire rack; painted pan with cover; measuring cup; measuring spoon; funnel; brush bottle cleaner; teething ring; extra diapers, and bubble pipe. Cindy Lee, SUN's 12-inch, drink-wet, jointed doll, wears a diaper and bib. Shipped ½ doz. in carton . . . Weight: 24 lbs.

© Ruth E. Newton

Betty Bows Baby Care Kit

© The Sun Rubber Co

No. 10631

All the paraphernalia necessary to lovingly care for an adorable doll is here in a new SUN carrying case set . . . Baby-sweet Betty Bows, the 12-inch sleeping doll with drink-wet-bubble blowing talents, is dressed in undershirt and panties . . . For dress-up occasions, there's a dress, slip, sunsuit, bib and bootees . . . To keep her clean and pretty, there's powder, soap, wash cloth, towel and extra diapers . . . A nursing bottle, bubble pipe, teething ring and hot water bottle provide extra fun . . . All are gift-appealingly arranged in a case so strong that it doubles as a little girls' traveling case . . . BABY CARE KIT is truly the most complete doll-care kit ever offered in the trade . . . Budget-minded shoppers will appreciate it because it means no extra-accessory buying. Shipped ¼ doz. per carton. Weight: 14 lbs.

212

Babee-Bee Carrying Case

© Ruth E. Newton

Babee-Bee CARRYING CASE

Equipped for full doll play the minute she arrives is Babee-Bee in her NEW Layette Set . . . This wonderful outfit includes the 13-inch, drink-wet, jointed doll with voice, vinyl head and long-lashed sleeping eyes . . . She wears an undershirt and panties under a long kimono . . . With her comes a wrinkle-free dress and slip, bootees, bib, weighing scales, plastic diaper bag, diaper, powder, soap, nursing bottle and bubble pipe . . . SUN's famous, sturdy, oval carrying case will also be proudly carried by little journeyers . . . Shipped ¼ doz. to carton . . . Weight: 16 lbs.

No. 10635

Top Summer Promotion and Lay Away Selections

213

Sun VINYL

the world's largest
rubber toy manufacturer
proudly introduces
its new Sunruco VINYL
toys and dolls

at the toy fair
818-22 hotel new yorker

THE SUN RUBBER COMPANY BARBERTON, OHIO

DRINK-WET BOTTLE BABIES

© Ruth E. Newton

"Betty Bows"

BOTTLE BABY

© The Sun Rubber Co.

No. 10027
"Babee-Bee"
Bottle Baby

© Ruth E. Newton

"Babee-Bee"

BOTTLE BABY

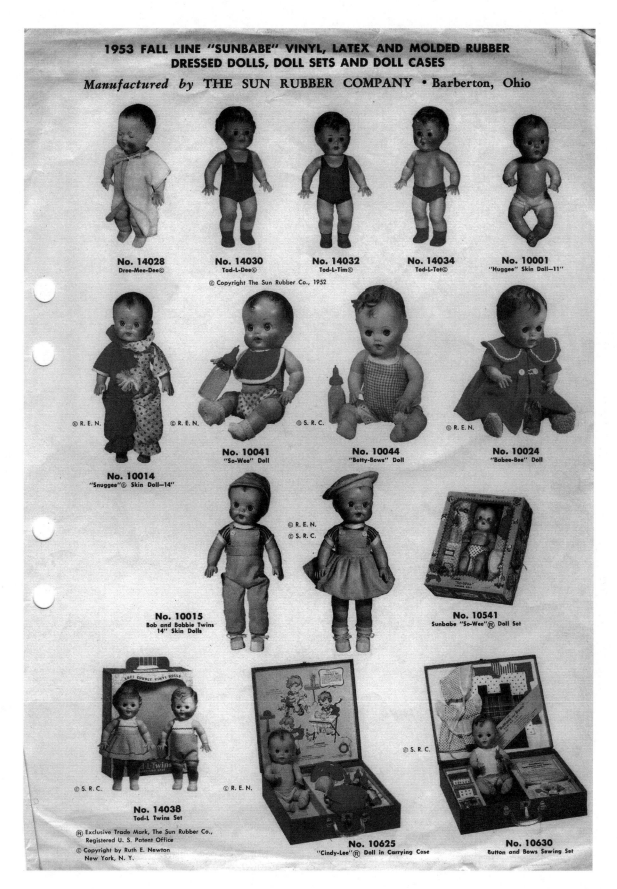

1953 FALL LINE "SUNBABE" VINYL, LATEX AND MOLDED RUBBER DRESSED DOLLS, DOLL SETS AND DOLL CASES

Manufactured by THE SUN RUBBER COMPANY • Barberton, Ohio

No. 14028
Dree-Mee-Dee©

No. 14030
Tod-L-Dee©

No. 14032
Tod-L-Tim©

No. 14034
Tod-L-Tot©

No. 10001
"Huggee" Skin Doll—11"

© Copyright The Sun Rubber Co., 1952

No. 10014
"Snuggee"© Skin Doll—14"

No. 10041
"So-Wee" Doll

No. 10044
"Betty-Bows" Doll

No. 10024
"Babee-Bes" Doll

No. 10015
Bob and Bobbie Twins
14" Skin Dolls

No. 10541
Sunbabe "So-Wee"® Doll Set

No. 14038
Tod-L Twins Set

® Exclusive Trade Mark, The Sun Rubber Co.,
Registered U. S. Patent Office
© Copyright by Ruth E. Newton
New York, N. Y.

No. 10625
"Cindy-Lee"® Doll in Carrying Case

No. 10630
Button and Bows Sewing Set

Twins Bob and Bobbie, pictured in the third row, are 14" skin dolls and difficult to find with their original costumes. The pair, with original clothes, is valued between $150-$195.

A Gallery of Dolls

All the dolls pictured in this section have been photographed from secondary market sources and from private collections. Rosemary and William Colter of the Dolls Store and More in Napa, California, deserve endless thanks for their cooperation.

A small collectible porcelain bride, only 6" tall, jointed. By Show Stoppers of Lakewood, New Jersey. Made in China stickers. Hand painted, hang tag. Value, $30-$35.

Katherine, by Robert Tonner, is a highly desirable Tonner doll. She is a stunning figure, made of vinyl with painted eyes in her exquisite face, and stands 21" tall. Her spectacular golden gown is covered with hand-sewn pearls, which match her pearl necklace and earrings. Maribou head piece, hang tag. Value, $650-$950.

Nettie is an "original sculpture" by Gustave F. Wolff. She is signed and numbered as indicated on the plaque on the stand which comes with the doll. The metal hang tag says, "Lexington Dolls Ltd. Hand painted, hand-sewn Porcelain Collector Dolls." She is 22" including the stand, and carries a basket, which in turn seems to harbor a furry little animal. She has delightful blue patent shoes, and her black curly hair compliments her dusky skin tone, and beautiful brown eyes. Her costume is adorable. She is wonderfully life-like and notice the expressive hands.
Value, $250-$350.

All shades of red hair are back in style. This auburn-tressed lovely is a musical ballerina. She is 18" tall and wears gold and white and ballet shoes. She is from the Broadway Collection and her head, hands, and feet are of high-fire bisque porcelain with an adorable hand-painted face. Value, $95-$150.

"Becky" is a beautiful doll from the Kingstate Prestige Collection. Her clothes and accessories are quite detailed, and her head is sculpted of fine bisque porcelain. She carries her own birthday cake replete with 5 candles (what an inspired 5th birthday gift for some lucky little girl), her hair color and wig are most attractive, and she wears fancy clothing. Even the shoes are nicely detailed with pearls and bows. Value, $150-$200.

This is Jordan, dressed in everyday cardigan sweater with big bold gold buttons over a yellow-print spring dress. Wide straw hat and metal hang tag. This is another exquisite doll by the talented Gustave F. Wolff, produced by Lexington Dolls Ltd.; $200-$300.

Ashton-Drake issued this doll by Michele Girard-Kassis, which commemorates Mother's Day in the most wonderful way. This doll is so life-like, the temptation is to engage her in conversation. She is a pink confection, with pink shoes, pink and white dress, and pink flower. She carries a card which says, I Love You Mom. Porcelain, hang tag. Value, $225-$325.

The dolls made by Show Stoppers are becoming more and more popular among collectors. Aisha is approximately 17" tall and wears pink and white, which highlights her dark curly hair. She is hand painted. Value, $100-$150.

Somehow, this doll looks exactly as a Jill should: A mischievous, fun-loving darling. Made of porcelain. Value, $150-$195.

This gorgeous doll is Sleeping Beauty, part of Ashton-Drake's Fairy Tale Princess series by Brigitte Duval, 1997. Everything about her—face, wig, tiara, dress, and pinafore certainly mark her as royalty. Value, $350-$450.

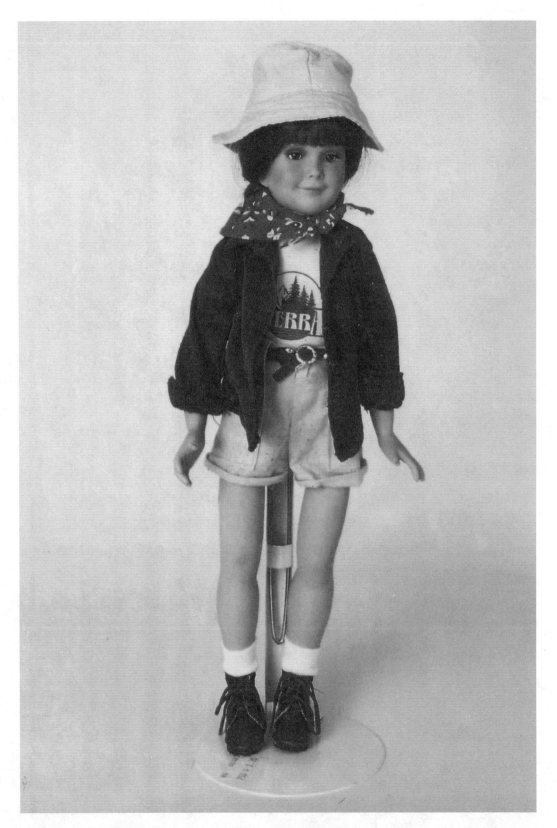

This doll represents somewhat of a departure in doll making. She was originally created to appeal exclusively to the outdoor girl and like most innovators, her maker began in a small way in California. She has an appealing expression and her costume reflects exactly what the doll maker intended her to be. She has a long single braid of hair not visible, and wears the uniform clothing necessary to hike or backpack in the Sierra Mountains. Her name, appropriately, is Sierra and she is somewhat scarce. Value, $175-$200.

Kingstate's Chin Chin is 20" of charm, wearing a colorful authentic-looking costume including velvet slippers. Made of porcelain, the doll is from the Prestige Collection. Value, $125-$145.

This Kais doll is full porcelain with a mohair wig. Approximately 26" tall, the doll wears an elabo-rate costume of pink chiffon and lace with red accents. Value, $400-$600.

This is a porcelain collector doll in the Wimbledon Collection by Lexington Dolls Ltd. Hand painted and hand sewn, this doll is named American Beauty, but unlike the typical long-legged American beauty, she is a diminutive figure, and her furs label her somewhat politically incorrect in today's society. She has the company's metal hang tag and carries an American beauty rose. Value, $55-$95

Daphne My Shoe Came Off is another beautiful doll by Gustave F. Wolff. Her winsome expression carries out the theme with great skill without lessening any of the impact. Her wig, clothing, and the plaque on the stand all point to the quality of the doll. It is signed and numbered. Hang tag-Lexington Dolls Ltd. Value, $275-$400.

Julietta, from Seymour Mann Doll Collector's Guild, is one of a limited edition of 2,500 by Eda Mann. Porcelain, hand painted, authentic costume. She has glass eyes, well-defined features, and is excellent quality. She is also quite striking and a lovely doll. Value, $200-$300.

A small Robert Tonner doll.

Marni, dressed as Cinderella, is one of Robert Tonner's Kripplebush Kids.

From the Connoisseur Collection by Seymour Mann, this doll has a lovely lavender shaded costume. Hand-painted porcelain, designed by Eda Mann. Approximately 22" tall. Value, $300-$400.

From the original sculpture by Gustave F. Wolff, this doll has the imposing designation, God Loves All Things Great and Small. Signed and numbered. Part of the Broadway Collection. Metal hang tag of Lexington Dolls Ltd. Plaque with information on base, which comes with doll; $350-$450.

Mikey Goes Camping is from the Wimbledon Collection of Lexington Dolls Ltd. Porcelain Collector Dolls. He is hand painted and hand sewn; $135-$175.

Winifred, part of the Dynasty Doll Collection, is approximately 25". Tinted porcelain-bisque parts are enhanced with hand-painted details. The company says only the "finest wigs, eyes, and accessories are used." The tag notes that this is imported by Cardinal Inc. of Port Reading, New Jersey, a division of Dynasty Dolls. A beautiful doll, its value is $325-$425.

A darling ringbearer, by the Dynasty Doll Collection. The costume is all white satin, and is appropriately charming. The young boy carries the requisite satin pillow, on which rest the two wedding rings. Approximately 14". Value, $125-$145.

A Georgetown Collection issue, this doll is in First Communion dress and wears a pretty cross to commemorate the day. She has wide-awake eyes, which reflect excitement at the event. She is approximately 16"; $150-$200.

This is Nancy the Bride. Many collectors are buying bride dolls, no matter who the maker or designer and no matter the basic material. There are now large collections of bridal dolls and they do make an impressive sight. They can also be a progressive fashion show of changing tastes. It is an interesting tangent of doll collecting, as more companies are producing bride dolls on a regular basis. Value, $75-$125.

Mother and Child, Prestige Collection of Kingstate Corp. The infant wears satin christening cloth-ing, the mother wears pink. Both of these faces are not only beautiful, but the mother's expression is highly evocative. Both figures, $250-$350.

Nurse Lola, from the Seymour Mann Connoisseur Collection. She would make anyone feel better, no doubt the reason her little bear doesn't seem to be suffering too much; $100-$200.

Myd is a Marian Hu doll of porcelain bisque. Her dolls have been marketed on TV, yet they have become somewhat scarce. This little scholar wears glasses and carries her notebook. Value, $125-$150.

Dynasty Dolls have become popular for some excellent reasons, primarily the appeal of the dolls themselves, the very emotional events they commemorate, the costuming, and, of course, quality. This is Annie. She carries her prayer book and also wears a cross as she goes off to church in her pink corduroy outfit, Sunday straw hat, and pristine white shoes. Value, $195-$250.

David, Heavenly Messenger, by Marlene Sirko. This is Kneeling David, part of a Nativity Set. Many collectors feel fortunate to find one of these figures. This is from the Artists' Edition, Georgetown Collection, and is 10". Made of bisque, this is a very popular doll. Value, $200-$225.

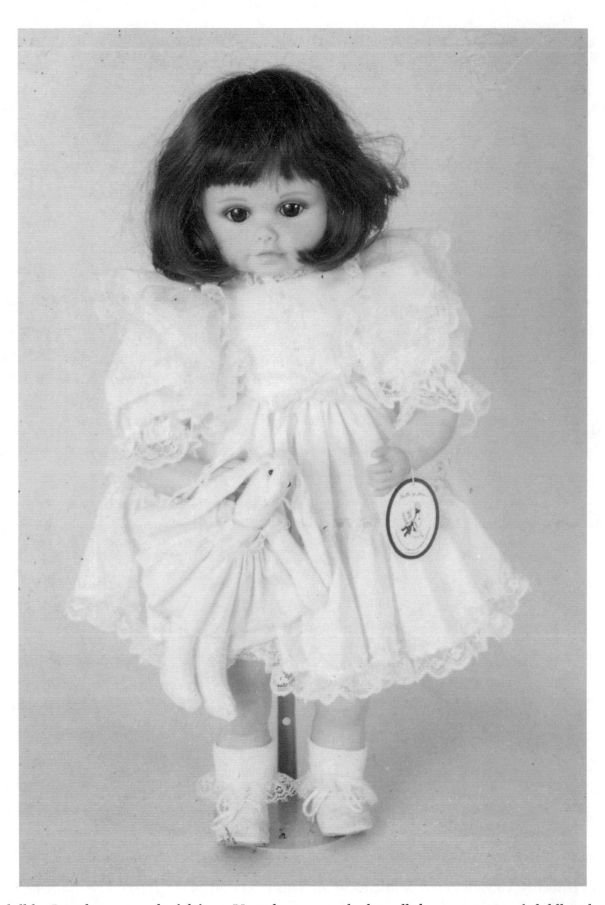

This doll by Jerri has a wonderful face. Katie by name, she has all the innocence of childhood, yet seems filled with curiosity. She has luminous glass eyes, is dressed in pink, and holds her toy rabbit. Value, $300-$500.

Jacqueline, by Duck House, is 20" tall. She wears a black and gold dress, gold beads, gold head band, gold slippers, and feather boa. Hang tag. Value, $95-$150.

Show Stoppers Inc. made this 16" porcelain beauty. Tag reads, "Hand made and hand painted."
She is "Musical Gina" and has a gorgeous costume of blue satin, laces, and bonnet.
Value, $150-$250.

A Delton Products Corp. collectible doll, Jilly has blonde curls, wears a blue and white striped dress, and carries her very own teddy bear. She is marked with the company logo on the back of the neck, and also has a hang tag. Her expression, with its open mouth, is a joy to behold. She seems the eternal child, seeking something new. Value, $195-$250.

School Daisy by Susan Wakeen, from the Susan Wakeen Doll Co., 1989. Made of vinyl, she wears a pinafore and has blue eyes behind the requisite scholar's eyeglasses; she also has a good looking school bag. A fine quality doll, she has great charm. Value, $350-$450.

This exquisite porcelain figure is from the Anna Collection by Dynasty Dolls. This series from Dynasty is quite beautiful and the costumes are superb. Down to the smallest detail, she exudes elegance. Her lace parasol, pearls, graceful gown and hat, combined with her lovely face, make this a very desirable doll. About 25" tall. Value, $400-$500.

Party Time by Duck House. She is, indeed, ready for a party with her sprightly red and white polka dot dress and big red bow, and her face literally beams with anticipation. She is a delight. Porcelain. Value, $100-$195.

Barbie achieving another goal: conquering the media as a world-famous songstress in slinky tight-fitting black. She is Solo in the Spotlight, which is almost always true, not matter what she is doing. Value, $50-$60.

Madam Alexander Fairy, from the Sleeping Beauty Collection. Impressively costumed as always, she is very attractive in her blue and gold. Value, $100-$125.

Mother and daughter, titled Mommy and Me on the Go, is an exciting duo by Madam Alexander from the Child's Play Collection. The visual appeal is stunning; these dolls are so contemporary in concept that 100 years from now, if still in original clothing, they will be used to explain fashions of the 1990s of the average working mother and her young daughter. Value of set, complete with accessories, $195-$225.

One of the Alexander "Classics" from the Sleeping Beauty Collection, this is the Evil Fairy, who looks much too adorable to be going about doing terrible things. Value, $95-$125.

The Coca Cola Collection by Alexander featured this car hop on roller skates. She really is the essence of that time and feeling. She has a sense of liveliness and appeals not only to doll collectors, but to collectors of Coca Cola memorabilia; 1997. Value, $125-$145.

This ballerina is from Madam Alexander's Ballet Collection. She is 21" tall and her beauty and quality can be experienced even from a photograph. Value, $175-$195.

This Guardian Angel doll by Alexander is from the Angel Collection. She is elaborately costumed and makes a striking addition to any collection of dolls or angels. With the new emphasis on collecting angels of any genre, this would be a welcome addition to such a collection. Value, $125-$150.

This is a doll from the Alexander Couture series. Value, $85-$100.

Gene, in diaphanous blue chiffon, is another beauty. These Gene dolls, while essentially glamorous fashion dolls, have great visual and emotional impact. They are well made and costumed in a provocative way, which at the same time is somewhat modest. Nel Odom, a very talented artist, made these for Ashton Drake. Value, $150-$195 and rising.

Madam Alexander's Kitty. She is a play doll and wears pink-dot tulle. Value, $125-$145.

Meg, one of the sisters in the classic children's book Little Women, *is from Madam Alexander's Journals Collection. Value, $100-$145.*

*Beth, another sister in Little Women, from Madam Alexander's Journals Collection.
Value, $100-$145.*

Madam Alexander's Scarlett, from the Storyland Series. Value, $250-$295.

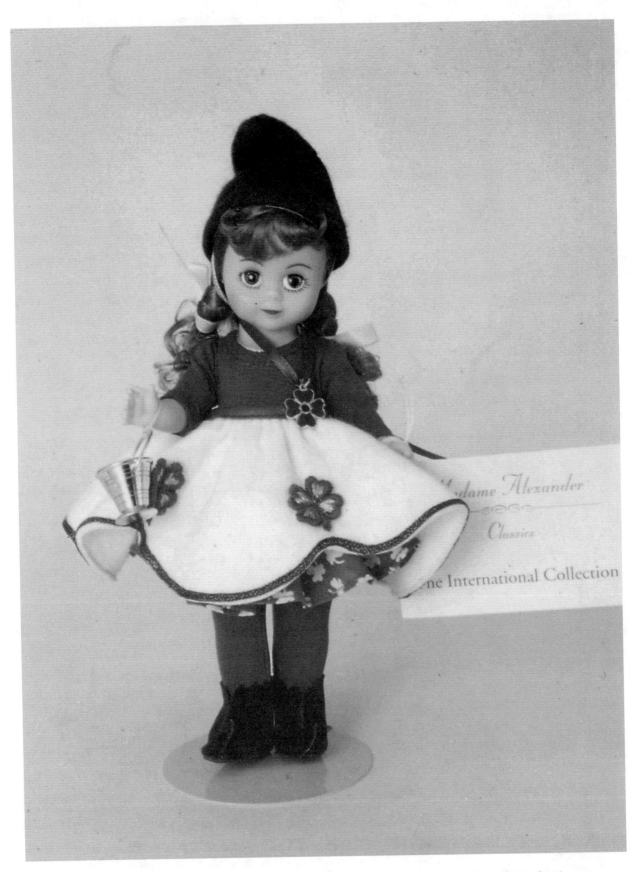

Irish Colleen, from the Madam Alexander International Collection. Value, $55-$85.

Gianni by Gotz (pronounced GOOD-TZ) is from the Designer Series. Made of vinyl, the doll has glass eyes and an open mouth, with bottom teeth visible. Made in Germany, hang tag is printed in German. Value, $200-$250.

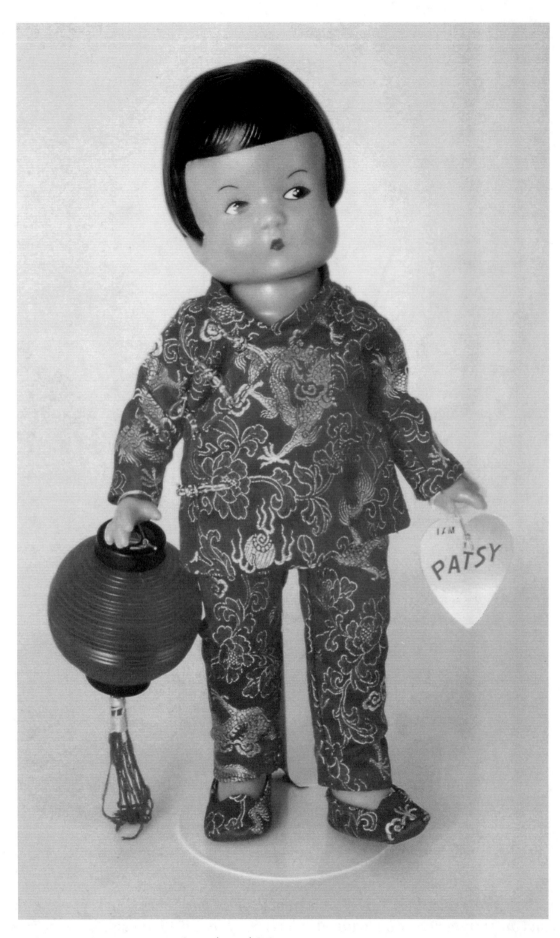

Effanbee's Chinese Patsy; 16". Value, $60-$75.

Cassandra is a beautifully made play doll by Gotz; $110-$145.

Although they are not dolls themselves, bears are a big part of doll collecting and any ones on the following pages would make an adorable addition to any doll collection. If one teddy is adorable, two can only be more so, especially when one is a baby bear. Belle and Baby, shown here, are original designs in mohair and have glass eyes. By Tucker Teddies. Value, $250-$295.

Virginia Jasmer, a well known Teddy Bear artist, made Pansy Bear, who certainly would be a unique, highly creative addition to a collection.

After all is said and done in the bear world, Yogi is still one of the most widely recognized in the world. The power of TV is at work here and all of these characters are a good investment. Yogi is made of all new materials with polyester fillers and wears the blue plastic tag on his ear. He also has a hang tag. By Applause Inc. and licensed by Hanna-Barbera, 1990. Value, in excellent condition with tags, $45-$50.

Doll collectors are seriously divided about the place in the world of Beanie Babies. There is no doubt, however, that any bear, Beanie or not, which commands hundreds, even thousands, of dollars deserves a place in the bear firmament. This is a completely volatile market in spite of the new price guides. The range is almost unbelievable, depending on location, availability, and your own desire to own one of these bears. This is Princess Bear, to whom the owner has added a regal tiara. Purple, she is THE Princess of course, has an applied rose, and the Ty Co. tag. The tag even has its own cover. The frenzy to obtain these bears rivals anything ever evidenced by the Cabbage-Patch craze. They keep escalating in price and who knows where it will all end. In perfect condition, with original tag, the value is around $35-$50, but has been known to climb as high as $300.

Erin Bear, with the applied shamrock, seems on the way to becoming more popular than Princess and in truth, he is adorable. Erin's value is around $45-$60, but also keeps rising as availability becomes a problem and could go as high as $300. Several price guides have already been published on Ty Beanie Babies, but these two examples are really rising stars and in this market, no guide can come close to a true evaluation. Values are unstable and most prices can range from $60 to many hundreds of dollars, even thousands.

Annette Funicello has endorsed a marvelous line of teddy bears. They are from the Collectible Bear, produced by Knickerbocker, which now owns the Georgetown Collection. Knickerbocker has always done superior work and these bears are no exception. Tiara is aptly named, except she sports not the usual tiara, but another little bear atop her head. By Christy Firkomage. Measures 17" tall. The issue price was $89, but the secondary-market prices have already risen to $125-$150 in some areas.

The beautiful boxes which house Annette Funicello bears are worthy of being collected on their own. No sensible person would discard such a box, but take special care of these; they are particularly lovely and Annette Funicello's signature will be important.

Here is a beautiful bear. Faith by name, it's 19" long and a delicious peachy-pink color. This is by Laura Dement. Any bear collector should hurry to add these; the beloved celebrity association will have great meaning and the bears are of fine quality and show imaginative designs. Value, $120-$175.

The Swan Princess, made of porcelain by Phyllis Parkins. Part of the Hamilton Collection. This is a large piece on its own stand, and can now be found only on the secondary market. A highly decorative item, as well as a beautiful doll. Value, $600-$800.

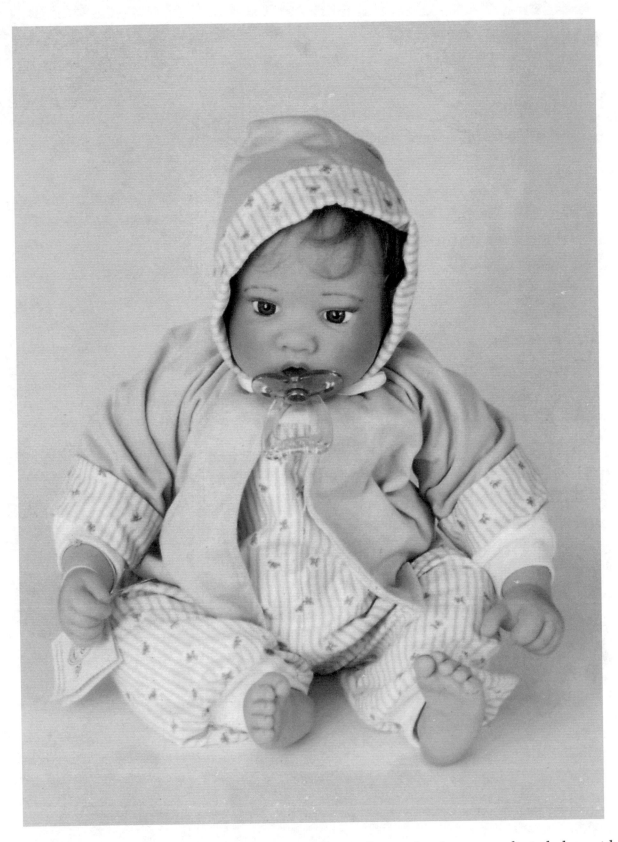

This baby doll, replete with pacifier, is by Lee Middleton Originals. A most realistic baby, with equally realistic clothing. Value, $175-$225.

New Ginny, as cute as ever in her car-hop uniform and roller skates, bubbles over with happiness as she prepares to take your order. Tag says, "Hi, I'm Ginny." Vogue Dolls, Oakdale, California. Value, $45-$55.

Dara, by Sissel Skile, is from the Georgetown Faraway Friends Collection, Artists Edition. Value, $125-$150.

A very perky Autumn is from the Wimbleton Collection, Lexington Dolls Ltd. Metal hang tag. Value, $175-$200.

The details on this doll are amazing. Poor Little Bo Peep has lost her sheep and two realistic tears are coursing down her cheeks. Fortunately, we know that all is well. By Wendy Lawton for Ashton-Drake, 1995. Value, $200-$300.

This is Michelle Valentine, by Lizzie High dolls. Made only for the Pasadena Bear and Doll show, she is a marvelous, endearing souvenir. Value, $125-$150.

Lavender and Lace by Dianna Effner, Ashton Drake, "What Are Little Girls Made of?" A very pretty doll and beautifully dressed; $145-$225.

This angel is by Cindy McClure. Winter Green is her name and she is from Victoria's Collectibles. Value, $300-$400.

Amy Plays in Nana's Attic is by Shirley A. Peck. Amy found a genuine mink scarf in that attic, which must be a treasure trove; $400-$500.

Lucy is from Crown Dolls, 1990, Artmark Co., Chicago, Illinois. Made of porcelain, this little darling also carries her pet teddy bear. Value, $125-$175.

Saying Grace, from Gorham, 1992. Porcelain. Both doll and bear are preparing to say grace before a meal and are already seated on a stool. Value, $250-$350.

One of the Friendship Series from Gorham, this is Peggy, the American Traveler, obviously ready to go. The doll, by Patricia Seamon, is a good example of the skills of the contemporary artists. The expression, clothing, and stance are all indicative of the theme of the doll. Value, $235-$350.

New Shoes is from the Hamilton Collection. The doll has the added value of the art work of Donna Zolan. It is fine bisque porcelain, hand painted, and dressed in hand-tailored clothing. Value, $300-$400.

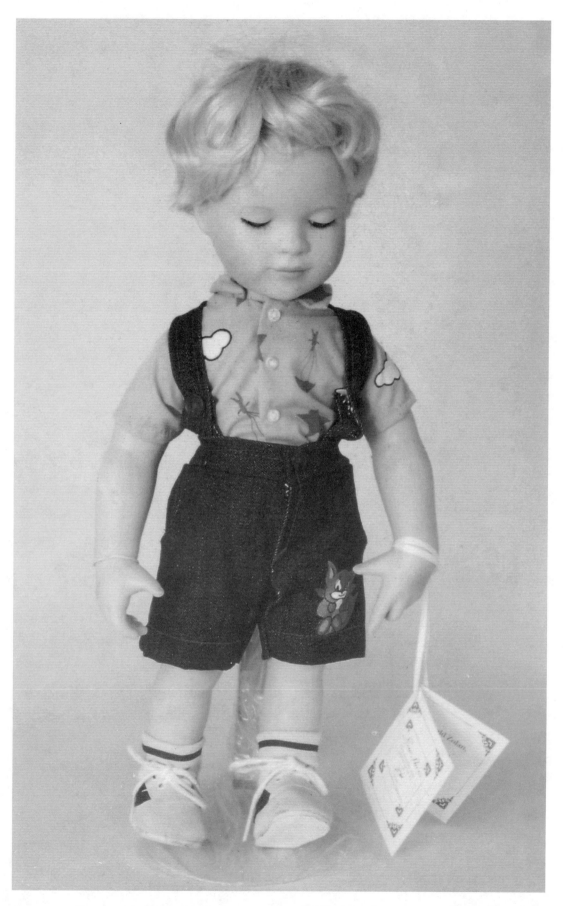

This Broadway-Collection doll has bisque head, hands, and feet, and a high-fire bisque porcelain, hand-painted face. All Broadway dolls come with a certificate of authenticity; $125-$195.

Delton Products Corp. made this small vinyl play doll. Value, $30-$40.

The gold Effanbee hang tag proclaims this adorable doll to be "durable." It is a remake of one of the older Effanbee successes. Measures 9" on stand; $27-$35.

If international dolls are your preference, don't neglect these well-done dolls from the D'Anton Range. The facial expressions are wonderfully life-like, the clothing is all suitable to the doll's activities, and all have well-defined hands and bare feet. Made in Spain; 10". Value, $55-$95.

These Zook Kids have "real eyes," a high-quality glass-like product which gives the illusion of the human eye, and changes color with changing light. Value, $150-$195.

A Jan Schackleford Originals Inc., these wonderfully crafted dolls are a family business and have the genuine folk-art look, which is so popular today. Value, $125-$135.

This is Small Fry, sitting in a metal chair and holding a baseball bat. These soft-bodied dolls are gaining popularity. The passion for "Americana" also enhances this market. Value, $35-$45.

Brigid, 1994, from Precious Moments; $125-$195.

North American Indian Doll Collection by Precious Moments. Even the hang tag on this is interesting. Huwuni, Apache; $125-$195.

Garden of Friends, by Precious Moments. These dolls are becoming very popular and the attention to detail by the company is evident. The hang tag is almost a collectible itself, it is so cute. Value, $95-$145.

D'Anton-Jos is a barefooted bundle of mischief from Spain. The company copyrighted these dolls in the United States in 1994. Measures 10". Value, $75-$125.

One of the great attributes of the D'Anton Range dolls is the mobile facial expressions. This little one, aside from her normal-looking clothing, is any child in action. This is a good area in which to start collecting. Value, $150-$195.

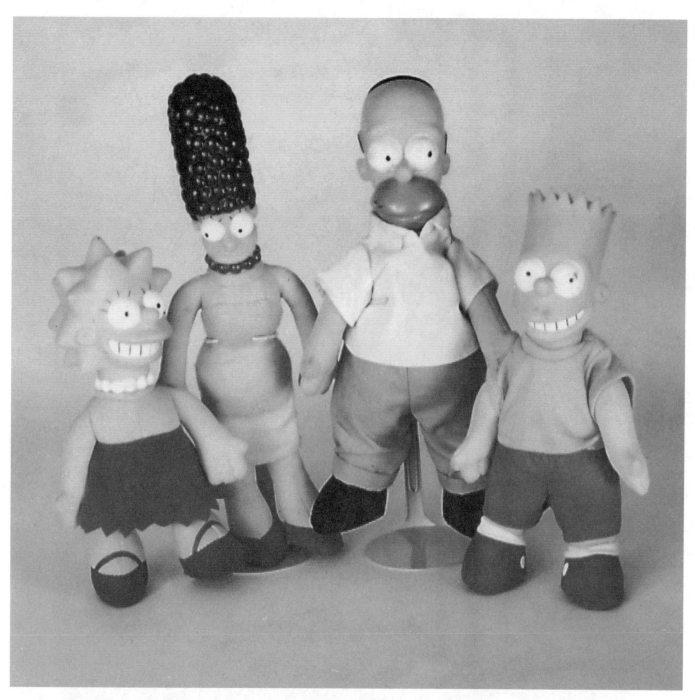

Here is the infamous Simpson family (minus baby Maggie), whose FOX TV show, "The Simpsons," has recently been listed as being among the most influential to American life in this decade. Individual characters are quite collectible and it is getting more difficult to find the whole family as a set. These figures come in various sizes, from tiny to quite large. The ones shown here measure 8-1/2" for Bart to 12" for Marge Simpson. All have labels which read, Matt Groening & 20th Century Fox FC 1990. As a set, $125-$145.

This Kingstate blonde cutie is Alice and she sits in her very own house. From the Fairy Tale Series, she is about 7". Value, $28-$35.

Sleeping Beauty in her very own personal castle. This attractive small doll is about 7". Kingstate. Value, $28-$35.

A beautiful toy set of pressed glass is a great addition to a doll collection. This is a complete set, but not all the pieces are shown here. The butter dish has a grape design in purple, and heavy gold trim. Value, $25; the sugar and creamer are $32.50 the set.

This new pressed-glass doll's set is a pretty accessory. The designs can vary on these, but this one has cherries with gold and is good-quality glass. The butter dish is valued at $20-$25; the sugar and creamer, $25-$30 for the set.

This little desk would certainly complement many of the new scholarly looking dolls being marketed. It is very well made in the old-style school desk and that tempting ink well is just made for dipping a long braid. Value, $30-$35.

This is March in the Months to Remember Series of Porcelain Collectible Dolls. Appropriate to her name, she is garbed in green. Russ. Value, $30-$35.

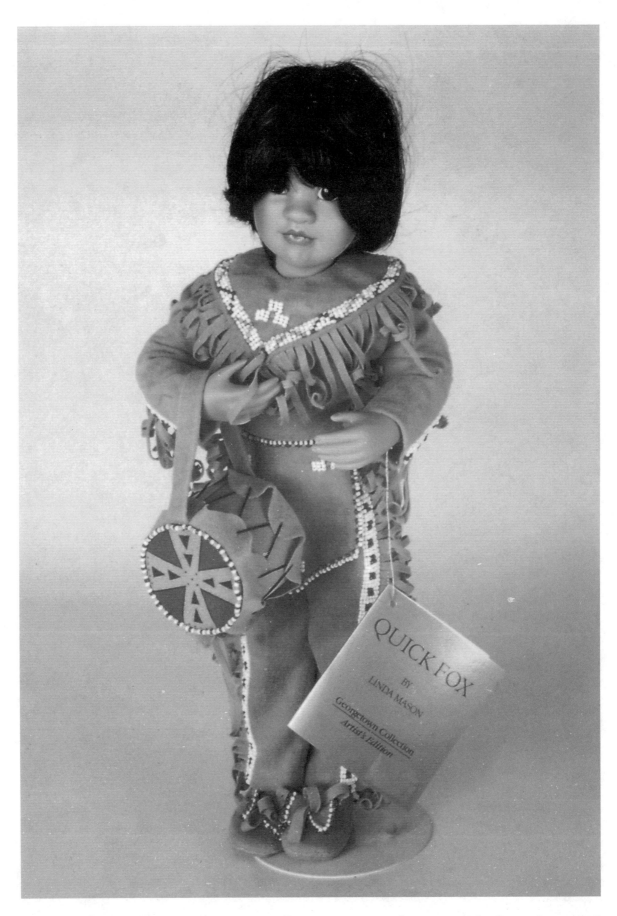

Quick Fox by Linda Mason, Georgetown Collection Artists Edition. Nicely dressed, impressive beading. All American-Indian artifacts, including dolls, are in great demand. Value, $135-$175.

Another Indian, this is by Duck House. "Indian Brave" has many accouterments, including a lovely small blanket. Value, $95-$145.

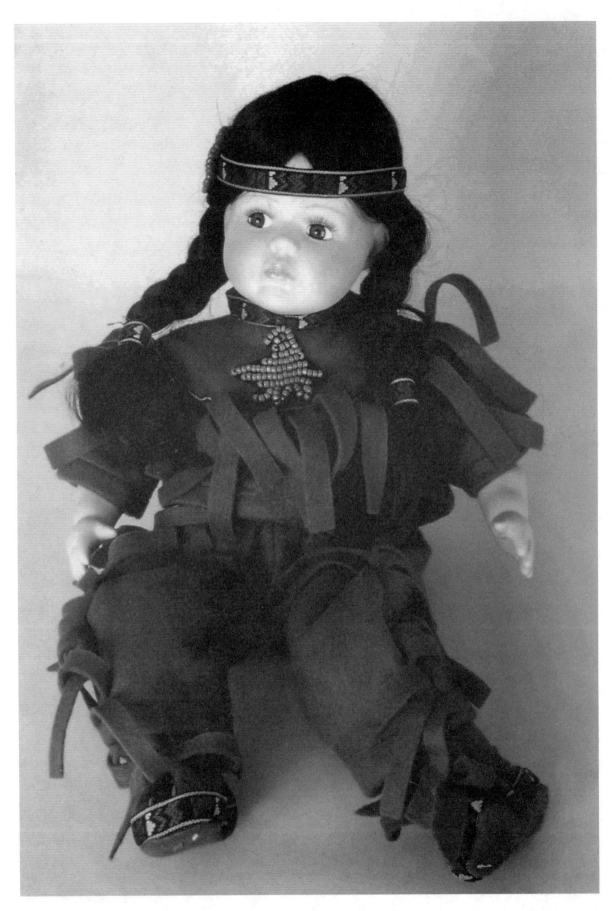

This Indian child is dressed all in felt, with some lovely beading. An authentic-looking costume, this is by an individual artist. Value, $75-$125.

A darling by Effanbee, "I Am Honey" is a wonderful copy of an earlier doll, even to the finish which resembles the old composition. Value, $125-$175.

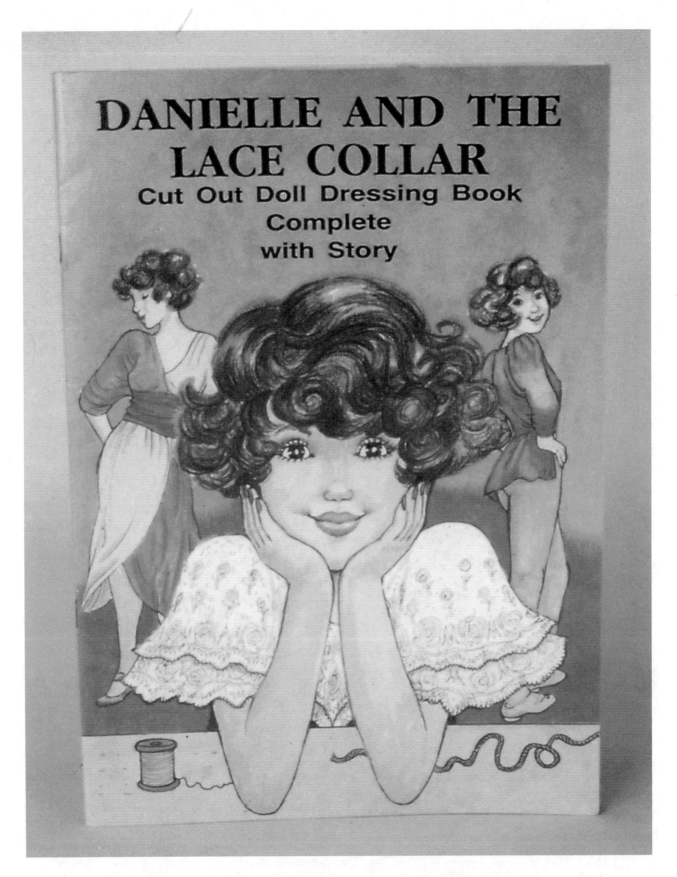

Danielle is an unusual paper-doll set, since she tells a story to fit the costumes. It was printed in Italy, for Peter Haddock Ltd., Birmingham, England. This, although in English, was bought in a bookstore in Brussels, Belgium, about 10 years ago, proving that no matter where you go, you may find your treasure. A different addition to a paper-doll collection, it has a value of $20-$25.

If you want to live with a constant smile on your face, put a picture of Miss Piggy where you can see it. This paper-doll set would do. She is here in all her glamorous glory ready to keep you happy, not only because that is her primary function, but because her paper-doll set by Colorforms is a coveted item and difficult to find. Value, $20-$22.

Lily is a walking, talking doll, but that's not all she does. Besides looking so delectable, she also sings "Farmer in the Dell." Lily is 2 feet tall, and has been restored. Her plastic shoes are interesting. Vinyl, 1940s; $180-$245.

A Miss-Revlon type. The owner/collector, who is very knowledgeable, hesitates to label her as a true Miss Revlon. She is a lovely doll in her pink-strapped dress. Made of vinyl, her value is $150-$185.

Terri Lee Brownie; vinyl. Value, $250-$275.

Marybell by Madam Alexander, 16", vinyl. Her vivid red dress has lacy trim, and the socks are also trimmed in red. Value, $250-$325.

Sweet Sue Toni Sophisticate, 1950s. Wig restored and replaced. Sleep eyes; 20".
Value, $225-$275.

Ideal's Saucy Walker, 1940s, vinyl. Value, $165-$200.

Teaching Teddy Prayers by Sandra Kuck, from the Hamilton Collection. A wonderful concept and a lovely doll. Value, $95-$150.

Adrianna, The Harvest Angel, is from the Little Bit of Heaven Collection, Artist's Edition. She has a porcelain face and cloth body.

Whatever it is about Raggedy Ann and Andy, Applause has certainly captured it here. This "re-creation" celebrates the birthday of the famous pair. Actually, Ann's original patent date was Sept. 7, 1915, while Andy's original patent date was Aug. 24, 1920. This doll here dates from 1987. Any artifacts relating to this pair should be acquired when found at any reasonable price, since they are becoming so popular prices are not rising, they are soaring. Value of Ann is $50-$95.

Andy, by Applause, is still in his original box. He is the other half of the famous duo and a companion to the Ann shown on the previous page. Applause Co. hang tag. Value, $50-$95.

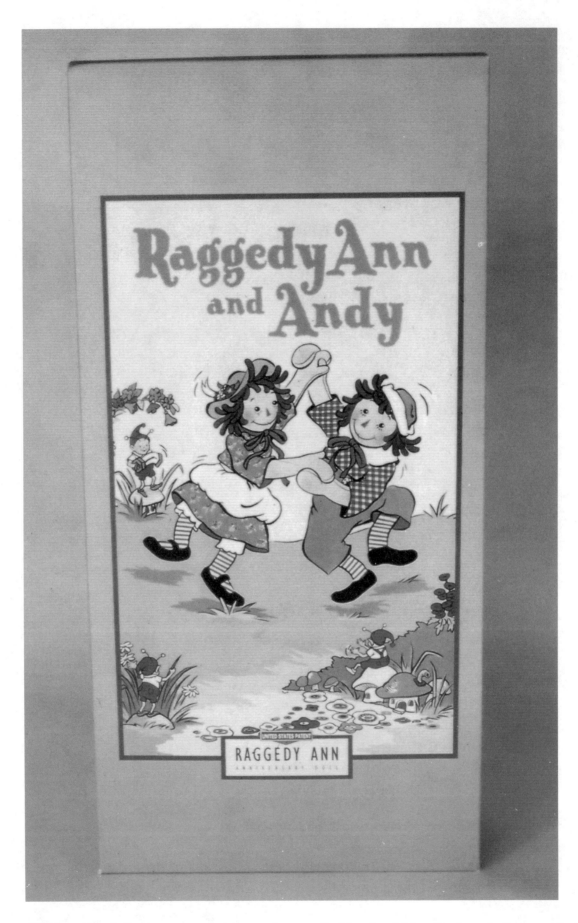

The boxes holding the dolls are so enchanting, they probably should be displayed along with the Ann and Andy dolls.

Aladdin, Step Into the World, is from Victoria's Collectible. These figures make tremendous decorative accents and as a collection, they are different and can be very exciting. Bisque porcelain; $35-$55.

Rabbits are a very close second to teddy bears among doll collectors, who also seem to adore these cuddly creatures. Actually, rabbits do make ideal pets and are becoming "in." There is no doubt that they are irresistible. Here is Jumpers, in striped pants and hat, by Russ Beri.
Value, $20-$30.

Jumpers' counterpart, Miss Buttons, is really lovable, and she carries her own lunch. Value, $20-$30.

A wonderful piece of folk art in the tradition of Ann and Andy, this is Prudence Penelope, holding tightly to her own doll. Heartfelt Collectibles; $45-$50.

*This Gotz doll, with her teddy-bear slacks, radiates with good health and good looks and exemplifies
"instant quality." It only takes one look to know you are looking at a high-quality doll. She has her
hang tag, and is valued between $150-$195.*

The Girl Golfer by Gotz, another play doll, shows the trend to sports dolls, which was quite popular for some time. The clothing of this doll is so exactly right and her golf bag so nicely made and stylish, she is the consummate lady golfer. Her cap is up to date and altogether she is a fine sports figure; $195-$250.

Here is Gotz' tennis player. This set of sports figures by this excellent manufacturer is a great bargain whatever the price. The concept is so contemporary, the costumes match the concept marvelously well, and the dolls themselves are very attractive. They are also play dolls, which is such a plus in today's market. This doll is wearing a stylish tennis outfit, which would easily wow Forest Hills. Her bag and racquet are the final wonderful touch; $195-$250.

If you are a fan of Victoriana, here is your rabbit. It's called Victorian Rose and the pink and lace, with the floral-decorated headpiece and trailing veil, will instantly plunge you back into Queen Victoria's time. The costume is so "in period," you will be charmed. Value, $50-$75.

Cissy, by Madam Alexander's Couture Collection. Actually, this is Cissy's Secret. The Alexander costuming is consistently beautiful. Matched with such a pretty face, this doll is irresistible. She comes with her own trunk and additional wardrobe. Value, $600-$800.

This baby girl, a play doll by Gotz, is not only cute and dressed in a most attractive way, it is machine washable. Soft body, 16". Value, $55-$75.

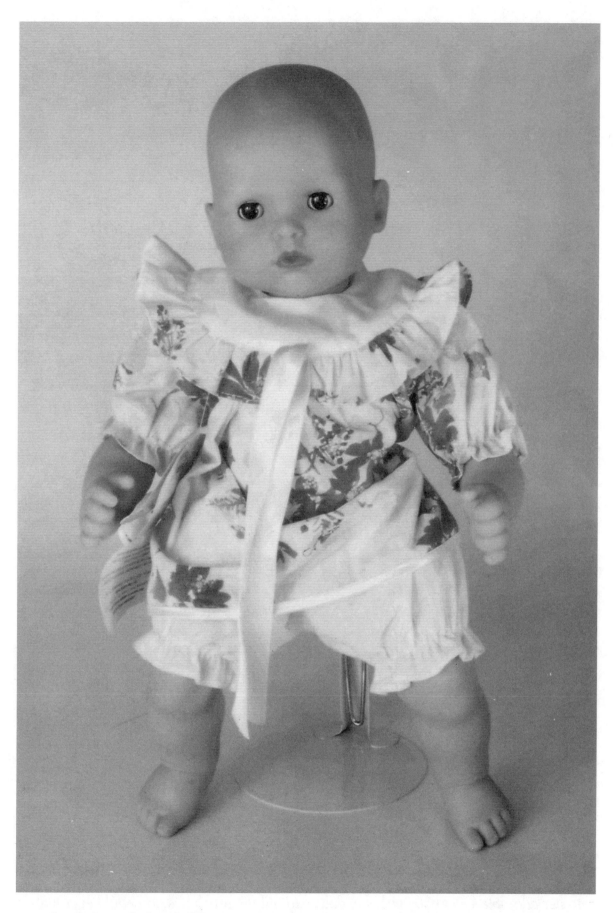

This is another baby girl play doll by Gotz. It is machine washable, has a soft body, and is 16".
Value, $55-$75.

This is another adorable Gotz baby girl play doll, with all the attributes you could ever want in a doll to be played with. She has a soft body to cuddle and simple clothes which can be machine washed, as can the doll itself. Measures 16". Value, $55-$75.

A full-porcelain doll, Valerie, by Dollmaker, has an exquisite face, lovely wig, and very contemporary-looking clothes. Value, $450-$550.

Charlotte, from the Dynasty Doll Collection, is 24" of Victorian regal elegance. Her muff and cape merely accentuate the basic fashion styling of this doll. Porcelain bisque parts, hand-painted details. Value, $250-$350.

An Anna Collection doll from Dynasty Dolls, you have to actually handle the clothing on this doll to realize its quality. First, of course, is the fashion aspect, then the fine fabrics, then the excellent bisque porcelain parts, and the well hand-painted details of the lovely face. As with any doll, the overall aspect has to considered. This series of Dynasty dolls really meet all qualifications for a high fashion, well-done doll. Measures 24". Value, $300-$400.

This dignified figure is Chief Gray Owl, a Sioux, by Sandy Dolls. This company issued an entire line of Indian dolls by Tribel. Vinyl. Value, $200-$300.

A rather winsome-looking Madam Alexander doll. The tag tells that "Cocoa Cola celebrates American Aviation." The doll wears aviator's goggles, her scarf blows in the wind, and she comes with her own paper plane. Value, $165-$195.

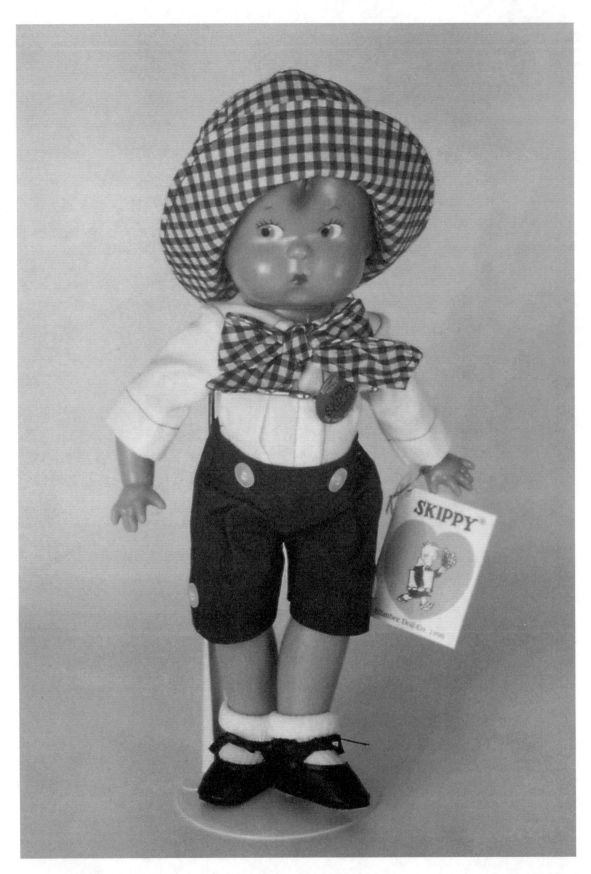

This is a re-issued Skippy, the 1920's comic-strip character created by P.L. Crosby, made in 1996 by Effanbee. He wears a button which says, "I am Skippy." Cute as ever, this was modeled from the original doll. He has side-glancing eyes, floppy hat, bow tie, and shorts. Made of vinyl, the doll is specially formulated to look and feel like the original composition. Value, $100-$200.

This small doll by Effanbee is 8" tall, made of vinyl and beautifully dressed in vintage style. Value, $45-$55

The heart tag on this Patsyette Autumn doll proclaims, "I am an Effanbee." This is a full-porcelain doll and is 10" tall. On her own stand, this new version explains why the original doll never lost popularity; $95-$145.

This remake of the original Patsy Joan is perky indeed in her blue and white sailor suit. Measures 16" and is made of vinyl. Value, $75-$95.

Heebie Sheebie is a Horseman reissue of an older composition doll. Both this doll and the one on the next page are wearing sailor suits, but this one has pink shoes. He-She dolls.
Value, the set, $100-$150.

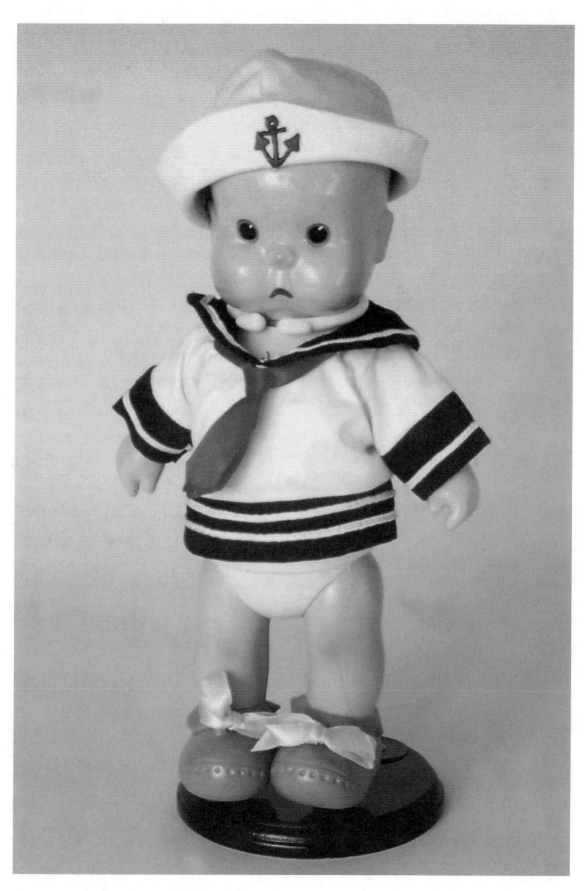

This Heebie-Sheebie wears blue shoes.

This is Effanbee's reissue of Patsyette Spring. It is truly amazing how dolls have changed and this one is a perfect illustration—she is nicely dressed, has lovely features and a well-formed body, but the look is so delightfully vintage. A great remake; $95-$150.

Glossary

Here are some important terms in the doll world:

Baby doll–Any doll made to represent an infant; regaining popularity.

Bisque–Unglazed porcelain, which is fired at very high temperatures. It can vary in shading from stark white to rosy pink.

Celluloid–A hard, flammable plastic. A trade name.

China–Porcelain which has been glazed; it can also vary in shading.

Composition–Blended wood fiber, paper, or sawdust and glue and sometimes other ingredients, which the manufacturers were reluctant to disclose. The hand painting of features on some composition dolls may contain lead-based paint. Small and large dolls were the simple designations given to dolls in the 1930s sold through popular catalogs–composition heads, legs, and arms.

Crazing–A term for cracking in composition dolls. Usually the result of too much heat or too much dampness. It is difficult to avoid in older dolls and if the damage is excessive, the doll should be restored only by a skilled professional.

Designer doll–Doll which carries the name of the artist who designed it. This is an increasingly important factor in contemporary doll collecting and can add appreciably to both price and collectibility.

Hang tag–The maker's or manufacturer's tag giving the pertinent information concerning the figure. This usually hangs from some part of the doll.

Jointed body–The ball-jointed bodies were made into the 1920s. These could be bent at certain joints in the doll body. This ability to move the knee and elbow joints is also called articulation.

MIB–Mint in Box. As dolls become more expensive and more widely collected, many are bought entirely for display or resale and are never removed from their original box. For resale, this is a great attraction.

Paperweight eyes–Usually blown glass which can have very human-like qualities.

Papier mâché–Short of mayhem, the papier-mâché doll is extremely durable. Each maker used slightly differing processes, but basically all involved paper pulp, size, paste, resin and sometimes other materials. All of these when mixed and still wet can be molded. The substance then hardens when dry. Some interesting dolls were made this way.

Pate–The crown of the doll's head. A removable piece, but the crown can also be solid. Important in older dolls.

Personality or celebrity dolls–These dolls are made in the likeness of some personality or celebrity with whom we have become familiar. Although usually through television or movies, many are cartoon characters or well known from other endeavors such as sports. This is a rising area of collecting.

Rag doll, or stuffed doll–These have been made practically forever. They are stuffed with various materials, including excelsior, cotton batting, fiber or anything that suits the purpose if they are crafted at home. Making a rag doll can be a very creative effort and some older ones are achieving great value.

PUT TO GOOD USE THE INFORMATION IN THESE BOOKS

1999 Toys & Prices
6th Edition
by Edited by Sharon Korbeck
The newest edition of the toy hobby's bible covers more than 18 categories of toys with detailed information and pricing in several grades of condition. New toy categories have been added bringing this edition to more than 19,000 toys dating from 1843 to 1997. As an added bonus, a toy manufacturers directory and an auction house list are included. Softcover • 6 x 9 928 pages • 500 b&w photos 20 color photos • **TE06 • $18.95**

New Edition

Luckey's Hummel Figurines & Plates
ID and Value Guide, 11th Edition
by Carl F. Luckey
Turn to this exhaustive volume for all your Hummel needs. More than 2,500 pieces - many shown in full color - include descriptions of color and mold variations, current production status and other remarks of interest for simple identification. You can put to good use the tips on recognizing fakes and forgeries and buying and selling for an enjoyable Hummel collecting experience. Softcover • 8-1/2 x 11 • 456 pages • 1123 b&w photos 16-page color section • **HUM11 • $24.95**

Sew the Essential Wardrobe for 18-Inch Dolls
by Joan Hinds & Jean Becker
Dress your doll for any occasion - from a holiday party to a workout at the gym. Create 18 modern outfits for today's popular 18-inch dolls such as: The American Girls Collection(r), Götz Dolls(r), Faithful Friends(r), and Storybook Heirlooms(r). Softcover • 8-1/4 x 10-7/8 96 pages • 250 Diagrams **EWD • $19.95**

Sewing & Sculpting Dolls
Easy-to-Make Dolls from Fabric, Modeling Paste and Polymer Clay
by Eloise Piper
Transform simple cloth dolls into lively characters with carefully-defined features. A basic cloth doll pattern is the basis for three "Sculpted" variations in beginning level with brushed-on gesso, intermediate with modeling paste and advanced with polymer clay. Softcover • 8-1/4 x 10-7/8 • 128 pages • color throughout **SSDED • $21.95**

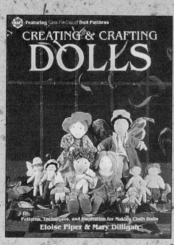

Creating & Crafting Dolls
Patterns, Techniques, and Inspiration for Making Cloth Dolls
by Eloise Piper & Mary Dilligan
Breathe life into your cloth dolls and give them personality of their own. Patterns, instructions, drawings for basic 12", 5" and 3" dolls include tips for creating skin tones, faces, hair styles and clothing. Ideal for beginning and experienced dollmakers alike. Softcover • 8-1/4 x 10-7/8 113 pages • color throughout • **CCD • $19.95**

Creative Dollhouses From Kits
by Robert Schleicher
Turning easy-to-build kits into custom dollhouses is a snap when you follow Robert Schleicher's step-by-step techniques. Learn to simulate clapboard siding; choose the right shingle; apply stucco, brick or stone; and install cornices and wallpaper. Softcover • 8-1/4 x 10-7/8 176 pages 16-page color section **CDFK • $19.95**